MznLnx

Missing Links Exam Preps

Exam Prep for

Managerial Accounting

Garrison, Noreen, & Brewer, 12th Edition

The MznLnx Exam Prep is your link from the texbook and lecture to your exams.
The MznLnx Exam Preps are unauthorized and comprehensive reviews of your textbooks.

All material provided by MznLnx and Rico Publications (c) 2010
Textbook publishers and textbook authors do not particpate in or contribute to these reviews.

MznLnx

Rico Publications

Exam Prep for Managerial Accounting
12th Edition
Garrison, Noreen, & Brewer

Publisher: Raymond Houge
Assistant Editor: Michael Rouger
Text and Cover Designer: Lisa Buckner
Marketing Manager: Sara Swagger
Project Manager, Editorial Production: Jerry Emerson
Art Director: Vernon Lowerui

Product Manager: Dave Mason
Editorial Assitant: Rachel Guzmanji
Pedagogy: Debra Long
Cover Image: Jim Reed/Getty Images
Text and Cover Printer: City Printing, Inc.
Compositor: Media Mix, Inc.

(c) 2010 Rico Publications
ALL RIGHTS RESERVED. No part of this work covered by the copyright may be reproduced or used in any form or by an means--graphic, electronic, or mechanical, including photocopying, recording, taping, Web distribution, information storage, and retrieval systems, or in any other manner--without the written permission of the publisher.

Printed in the United States
ISBN:

For more information about our products, contact us at:
Dave.Mason@RicoPublications.com

For permission to use material from this text or product, submit a request online to:
Dave.Mason@RicoPublications.com

Contents

CHAPTER 1
One Managerial Accounting and the Business Environment — 1

CHAPTER 2
Two Cost Terms, Concepts, and Classifications — 16

CHAPTER 3
Three Systems Design: Job-Order Costing — 27

CHAPTER 4
Four Systems Design: Process Costing — 33

CHAPTER 5
Five Cost Behavior: Analysis and Use — 38

CHAPTER 6
Six Cost-Volume-Profit Relationships — 42

CHAPTER 7
Seven Variable Costing: A Tool for Management — 46

CHAPTER 8
Eight Activity-Based Costing: A Tool to Aid Decision Making — 52

CHAPTER 9
Nine Profit Planning — 56

CHAPTER 10
Ten Standard Costs and the Balanced Scorecard — 61

CHAPTER 11
Eleven Flexible Budgets and Overhead Analysis — 69

CHAPTER 12
Twelve Segment Reporting and Decentralization — 72

CHAPTER 13
Thirteen Relevant Costs for Decision Making — 86

CHAPTER 14
Fourteen Capital Budgeting Decisions — 95

CHAPTER 15
Fifteen "How Well Am I Doing?" Statement of Cash Flows — 108

CHAPTER 16
Sixteen "How Well Am I Doing?" Financial Statement Analysis — 114

ANSWER KEY — 132

TO THE STUDENT

COMPREHENSIVE

The *MznLnx* Exam Prep series is designed to help you pass your exams. Editors at MznLnx review your textbooks and then prepare these practice exams to help you master the textbook material. Unlike study guides, workbooks, and practice tests provided by the texbook publisher and textbook authors, *MznLnx* gives you **all** of the material in each chapter in exam form, not just samples, so you can be sure to nail your exam.

MECHANICAL

The MznLnx Exam Prep series creates exams that will help you learn the subject matter as well as test you on your understanding. Each question is designed to help you master the concept. Just working through the exams, you gain an understanding of the subject--its a simple mechanical process that produces success.

INTEGRATED STUDY GUIDE AND REVIEW

MznLnx is not just a set of exams designed to test you, its also a comprehensive review of the subject content. Each exam question is also a review of the concept, making sure that you will get the answer correct without having to go to other sources of material. You learn as you go! Its the easiest way to pass an exam.

HUMOR

Studying can be tedious and dry. MznLnx's instructional design includes moderate humor within the exam questions on occassion, to break the tedium and revitalize the brain

Chapter 1. One Managerial Accounting and the Business Environment

1. The _____ is a private, not-for-profit organization whose primary purpose is to develop generally accepted accounting principles (GAAP) within the United States in the public's interest. The Securities and Exchange Commission (SEC) designated the _____ as the organization responsible for setting accounting standards for public companies in the U.S. It was created in 1973, replacing the Accounting Principles Board and the Committee on Accounting Procedure of the American Institute of Certified Public Accountants. The _____'s mission is 'to establish and improve standards of financial accounting and reporting for the guidance and education of the public, including issuers, auditors, and users of financial information.'

The _____ is not a governmental body.

   a. Fannie Mae
   b. Public company
   c. Governmental Accounting Standards Board
   d. Financial Accounting Standards Board

2. _____ is the term used to refer to the standard framework of guidelines for financial accounting used in any given jurisdiction. _____ includes the standards, conventions, and rules accountants follow in recording and summarizing transactions, and in the preparation of financial statements.

Financial accounting information must be assembled and reported objectively.

   a. Long-term liabilities
   b. Current asset
   c. General ledger
   d. Generally accepted accounting principles

3. _____ is concerned with the provisions and use of accounting information to managers within organizations, to provide them with the basis to make informed business decisions that will allow them to be better equipped in their management and control functions.

In contrast to financial accountancy information, _____ information is:

   - usually confidential and used by management, instead of publicly reported;
   - forward-looking, instead of historical;
   - pragmatically computed using extensive management information systems and internal controls, instead of complying with accounting standards.

This is because of the different emphasis: _____ information is used within an organization, typically for decision-making.

a. Governmental accounting
b. Grenzplankostenrechnung
c. Management accounting
d. Nonassurance services

4. The _____ is a trilateral trade bloc in North America created by the governments of the United States, Canada, and Mexico. The agreement creating the trade bloc came into force on January 1, 1994. It superseded the Canada-United States Free Trade Agreement between the U.S. and Canada.

a. North American Free Trade Agreement
b. Collusion
c. Moving average
d. Chief executive officer

5. An _____ is a practitioner of accountancy, which is the measurement, disclosure or provision of assurance about financial information that helps managers, investors, tax authorities and other decision makers make resource allocation decisions.

The word '_____' is derived from the French 'Compter' which took its origin from the Latin 'Computare'. The word was formerly written in English as 'Accomptant', but in process of time the word, which was always pronounced by dropping the 'p', became gradually changed both in pronunciation and in orthography to its present form.

a. ABC Television Network
b. AIG
c. AMEX
d. Accountant

6. _____ is a costing model that identifies activities in an organization and assigns the cost of each activity resource to all products and services according to the actual consumption by each: it assigns more indirect costs (overhead) into direct costs.

In this way an organization can establish the true cost of its individual products and services for the purposes of identifying and eliminating those which are unprofitable and lowering the prices of those which are overpriced.

In a business organization, the ABC methodology assigns an organization's resource costs through activities to the products and services provided to its customers.

Chapter 1. One Managerial Accounting and the Business Environment

a. Activity-based costing
b. ABC Television Network
c. Activity-based management
d. Indirect costs

7. The title _____ is a professional designation awarded by various professional bodies around the world.

The _____ designation is a post-nominal award issued to individuals who have achieved a peer-based criteria of professional competency in the field of Management Accounting. Management accounting qualifications differ from those such as the ACA or CPA 'Chartered' or 'Public' accounting qualifications in a number of ways.

a. Convey Compliance Systems
b. 3M Company
c. BMC Software, Inc.
d. Certified management accountant

8. _____ are formal records of a business' financial activities.

In British English, including United Kingdom company law, _____ are often referred to as accounts, although the term _____ is also used, particularly by accountants.

_____ provide an overview of a business' financial condition in both short and long term.

a. Statement of retained earnings
b. Financial statements
c. Notes to the financial statements
d. 3M Company

9. A _____, also client, buyer or purchaser is the buyer or user of the paid products of an individual or organization, mostly called the supplier or seller. This is typically through purchasing or renting goods or services.

a. BMC Software, Inc.
b. 3M Company
c. BNSF Railway
d. Customer

Chapter 1. One Managerial Accounting and the Business Environment

10. _____, commonly known as e-commerce or eCommerce, consists of the buying and selling of products or services over electronic systems such as the Internet and other computer networks. The amount of trade conducted electronically has grown extraordinarily since the spread of the Internet. A wide variety of commerce is conducted in this way, spurring and drawing on innovations in electronic funds transfer, supply chain management, Internet marketing, online transaction processing, electronic data interchange (EDI), inventory management systems, and automated data collection systems.
   a. AIG
   b. ABC Television Network
   c. Electronic commerce
   d. Electronic data interchange

11. _____ is a demonstration of a process -- such as a variable, term, or object -- relative in terms of the specific process or set of validation tests used to determine its presence and quantity. Properties described in this manner must be sufficiently accessible, so that persons other than the definer may independently measure or test for them at will. An _____ is generally designed to model a conceptual definition.
   a. ABC Television Network
   b. AIG
   c. AMEX
   d. Operational definition

12. In cost-volume-profit analysis, a form of management accounting, _____ is the marginal profit per unit sale. It is a useful quantity in carrying out various calculations, and can be used as a measure of operating leverage.

The Total _____ is Total Revenue (TR, or Sales) minus Total Variable Cost (TVC):

   Tcontribution margin = TR − TVC

The Unit _____ (C) is Unit Revenue (Price, P) minus Unit Variable Cost (V):

   C = P − V

The _____ Ratio is the percentage of Contribution over Total Revenue, which can be calculated from the unit contribution over unit price or total contribution over Total Revenue:

$$\frac{C}{P} = \frac{P-V}{P} = \frac{\text{Unit Contribution Margin}}{\text{Price}} = \frac{\text{Total Contribution Margin}}{\text{Total Revenue}}$$

For instance, if the price is $10 and the unit variable cost is $2, then the unit _____ is $8, and the _____ ratio is $8/$10 = 80%.

a. Factory overhead
b. Cost management
c. Contribution margin
d. Profit center

13. _____ describes the situation when output from (or information about the result of) an event or phenomenon in the past will influence the same event/phenomenon in the present or future. When an event is part of a chain of cause-and-effect that forms a circuit or loop, then the event is said to 'feed back' into itself.

_____ is also a synonym for:

- _____ Signal; the information about the initial event that is the basis for subsequent modification of the event.
- _____ Loop; the causal path that leads from the initial generation of the _____ signal to the subsequent modification of the event.

_____ is a mechanism, process or signal that is looped back to control a system within itself. Such a loop is called a _____ loop.

a. BMC Software, Inc.
b. 3M Company
c. Controllable
d. Feedback

14. Government _____ are designed to show nonfinancial aspects of government operations. For example, a government financial report might include the number of arrests, number of convictions by crime category as well as the change (i.e., increase or decrease) in crime rate. Government _____ usually provide data on environmental conditions, education and conditions of streets and roads.
a. Performance reports
b. BNSF Railway
c. 3M Company
d. BMC Software, Inc.

15. A _____ is a fungible, negotiable instrument representing financial value. they are broadly categorized into debt securities (such as banknotes, bonds and debentures), and equity securities; e.g., common stocks. The company or other entity issuing the _____ is called the issuer.

Chapter 1. One Managerial Accounting and the Business Environment

a. Tracking stock
b. BMC Software, Inc.
c. 3M Company
d. Security

16. The U.S. _____ is an independent agency of the United States government which holds primary responsibility for enforcing the federal securities laws and regulating the securities industry, the nation's stock and options exchanges, and other electronic securities markets. The SEC was created by section 4 of the Securities Exchange Act of 1934 (now codified as 15 U.S.C. §§ 78d and commonly referred to as the 1934 Act.)
a. Securities and Exchange Commission
b. 3M Company
c. BMC Software, Inc.
d. BNSF Railway

17. An _____ is a mostly hierarchical concept of subordination of entities that collaborate and contribute to serve one common aim.

Organizations are a variant of clustered entities. The structure of an organization is usually set up in many a styles, dependent on their objectives and ambience.

a. AIG
b. ABC Television Network
c. AMEX
d. Organizational structure

18. The _____ of a company or public agency is the corporate officer primarily responsible for managing the financial risks of the business or agency. This officer is also responsible for financial planning and record-keeping, as well as financial reporting to higher management. (In recent years, however, the role has expanded to encompass communicating financial performance and forecasts to the analyst community.)
a. Merck ' Co., Inc.
b. Chief executive officer
c. NASDAQ
d. Chief Financial Officer

19. The _____ is a concept from business management that was first described and popularized by Michael Porter in his 1985 best-seller, Competitive Advantage: Creating and Sustaining Superior Performance.

A _____ is a chain of activities. Products pass through all activities of the chain in order and at each activity the product gains some value.

a. Product differentiation
b. Value chain
c. Customer relationship management
d. Market segmentation

20. _____s are goods that have completed the manufacturing process but have not yet been sold or distributed to the end user.

Manufacturing has three classes of inventory:

1. Raw material
2. Work in process
3. _____s

A good purchased as a 'raw material' goes into the manufacture of a product. A good only partially completed during the manufacturing process is called 'work in process'. When the good is completed as to manufacturing but not yet sold or distributed to the end-user is called a '_____'.

a. Reorder point
b. FIFO and LIFO accounting
c. 3M Company
d. Finished good

21. Lean manufacturing or _____, which is often known simply as 'Lean', is a production practice that considers the expenditure of resources for any goal other than the creation of value for the end customer to be wasteful, and thus a target for elimination. Working from the perspective of the customer who consumes a product or service, 'value' is defined as any action or process that a customer would be willing to pay for. Basically, lean is centered around creating more value with less work.
a. Six Sigma
b. Lean manufacturing
c. Make to order
d. Lean production

Chapter 1. One Managerial Accounting and the Business Environment

22. A _____ is something that is acted upon or used by or by human labour or industry, for use as a building material to create some product or structure. Often the term is used to denote material that came from nature and is in an unprocessed or minimally processed state. Iron ore, logs, and crude oil, would be examples.
    a. BNSF Railway
    b. Raw material
    c. 3M Company
    d. BMC Software, Inc.

23. _____ or in-process inventory includes the set at large of unfinished items for products in a production process. These items are not yet completed but either just being fabricated or waiting in a queue for further processing or in a buffer storage. The term is used in production and supply chain management.
    a. 3M Company
    b. BMC Software, Inc.
    c. Work in process
    d. BNSF Railway

24. Just in Time could refer to the following:

    - _____, an inventory strategy that reduces in-process inventory
    - _____ compilation, a technique for improving the performance of bytecode-compiled programming systems

    a. Just-in-time
    b. Comparable
    c. Help desk and incident reporting auditing
    d. Fiscal

25. Procter is a surname, and may also refer to:

    - Bryan Waller Procter (pseud. Barry Cornwall), English poet
    - Goodwin Procter, American law firm
    - _____, consumer products multinational

    a. Screening
    b. Procter ' Gamble
    c. Welfare
    d. Markup

Chapter 1. One Managerial Accounting and the Business Environment

26. A '_____ is the system of organizations, people, technology, activities, information and resources involved in moving a product or service from supplier to customer. _____ activities transform natural resources, raw materials and components into a finished product that is delivered to the end customer. In sophisticated _____ systems, used products may re-enter the _____ at any point where residual value is recyclable.
   a. Consignor
   b. Supply chain
   c. Free port
   d. Purchasing

27. _____ is an overall management philosophy introduced by Dr. Eliyahu M. Goldratt in his 1984 book titled The Goal, that is geared to help organizations continually achieve their goal. The title comes from the contention that any manageable system is limited in achieving more of its goal by a very small number of constraints, and that there is always at least one constraint. The _____ process seeks to identify the constraint and restructure the rest of the organization around it, through the use of the Five Focusing Steps.
   a. Lean production
   b. Theory of Constraints
   c. Six Sigma
   d. Lean manufacturing

28. _____ is a business management strategy, initially implemented by Motorola, that today enjoys widespread application in many sectors of industry.

_____ seeks to improve the quality of process outputs by identifying and removing the causes of defects (errors) and variation in manufacturing and business processes. It uses a set of quality management methods, including statistical methods, and creates a special infrastructure of people within the organization ('Black Belts' etc.)

   a. Make to order
   b. Lean manufacturing
   c. Theory of constraints
   d. Six Sigma

29. In financial and business accounting, _____ is a measure of a firm's profitability that excludes interest and income tax expenses.

EBIT = Operating Revenue - Operating Expenses (OPEX) + Non-operating Income

Operating Income = Operating Revenue - Operating Expenses

Operating income is the difference between operating revenues and operating expenses, but it is also sometimes used as a synonym for EBIT and operating profit. This is true if the firm has no non-operating income.

a. AIG
b. ABC Television Network
c. AMEX
d. Earnings before interest and taxes

30. _____ is a specific term used in companies' financial reporting from the company-whole point of view. Because that use excludes the effects of changing ownership interest, an economic measure of _____ is necessary for financial analysis from the shareholders' point of view

_____ is defined by the Financial Accounting Standards Board, or FASB, as 'the change in equity [net assets] of a business enterprise during a period from transactions and other events and circumstances from nonowner sources. It includes all changes in equity during a period except those resulting from investments by owners and distributions to owners.'

_____ is the sum of net income and other items that must bypass the income statement because they have not been realized, including items like an unrealized holding gain or loss from available for sale securities and foreign currency translation gains or losses.

a. 3M Company
b. BMC Software, Inc.
c. Comprehensive income
d. BNSF Railway

31. Project _____: The project _____ is a prediction of the costs associated with a particular company project. These costs include labor, materials, and other related expenses. The project _____ is often broken down into specific tasks, with task _____s assigned to each.
a. 3M Company
b. Budget
c. BNSF Railway
d. BMC Software, Inc.

32. _____ is a fee paid on borrowed assets. It is the price paid for the use of borrowed money, or, money earned by deposited funds .Assets that are sometimes lent with _____ include money, shares, consumer goods through hire purchase, major assets such as aircraft, and even entire factories in finance lease arrangements. The _____ is calculated upon the value of the assets in the same manner as upon money.

Chapter 1. One Managerial Accounting and the Business Environment

a. AIG
b. Interest
c. Insolvency
d. ABC Television Network

33. _____ consists of the processes a company uses to track and organize its contacts with its current and prospective customers. _____ software is used to support these processes; information about customers and customer interactions can be entered, stored and accessed by employees in different company departments. Typical _____ goals are to improve services provided to customers, and to use customer contact information for targeted marketing.
   a. Value chain
   b. Market segmentation
   c. Market share
   d. Customer relationship management

34. _____ is a company-wide computer software system used to manage and coordinate all the resources, information, and functions of a business from shared data stores.

An _____ system has a service-oriented architecture with modular hardware and software units or 'services' that communicate on a local area network. The modular design allows a business to add or reconfigure modules (perhaps from different vendors) while preserving data integrity in one shared database that may be centralized or distributed.

   a. AMEX
   b. Enterprise Resource Planning
   c. ABC Television Network
   d. AIG

35. _____ in business includes the methods and processes used by organizations to manage risks and seize opportunities related to the achievement of their objectives. _____ provides a framework for risk management, which typically involves identifying particular events or circumstances relevant to the organization's objectives (risks and opportunities), assessing them in terms of likelihood and magnitude of impact, determining a response strategy, and monitoring progress. By identifying and proactively addressing risks and opportunities, business enterprises protect and create value for their stakeholders, including owners, employees, customers, regulators, and society overall.
   a. Enterprise risk management
   b. ABC Television Network
   c. AMEX
   d. AIG

Chapter 1. One Managerial Accounting and the Business Environment

36. _____ is a concept that denotes the precise probability of specific eventualities. Technically, the notion of _____ is independent from the notion of value and, as such, eventualities may have both beneficial and adverse consequences. However, in general usage the convention is to focus only on potential negative impact to some characteristic of value that may arise from a future event.
    a. Risk
    b. Risk adjusted return on capital
    c. Discount factor
    d. Discounting

37. _____ is activity directed towards the assessing, mitigating (to an acceptable level) and monitoring of risks. In some cases the acceptable risk may be near zero. Risks can come from accidents, natural causes and disasters as well as deliberate attacks from an adversary.
    a. Kanban
    b. Trademark
    c. FIFO
    d. Risk management

38. The _____ is a professional organization headquartered in Montvale, New Jersey consisting of over 70,000 members worldwide. The IMA is dedicated to advancing the role of the management accountant and financial manager within the business organization, and provides relevant professional certification.

The IMA awards the Certified Management Accountant (CMA) designation in the United States.

    a. Emerging technologies
    b. Institute of Management Accountants
    c. International Accounting Standards Committee
    d. American Accounting Association

39. The _____ is the global organization for the accountancy profession. IFAC has 157 member bodies and associates in 123 countries and jurisdictions, representing more than 2.5 million accountants employed in public practice, industry and commerce, government, and academe. The organization, through its independent standard-setting boards, establishes international standards on ethics, auditing and assurance, education, and public sector accounting.
    a. American Payroll Association
    b. International Federation of Accountants
    c. Emerging technologies
    d. International Accounting Standards Committee

Chapter 1. One Managerial Accounting and the Business Environment 13

40. The _____ is the national, professional association of CPAs in the United States, with more than 330,000 members, including CPAs in business and industry, public practice, government, and education; student affiliates; and international associates. It sets ethical standards for the profession and U.S. auditing standards for audits of private companies; federal, state and local governments; and non-profit organizations.

Approximately 40% of its members are engaged in the practice of public accounting, in areas such as auditing, accounting, taxation, general business consulting, business valuation, personal financial planning and business technology.

   a. AIG
   b. American Institute of Certified Public Accountants
   c. Other postemployment benefits
   d. ABC Television Network

41. _____ is the statutory title of qualified accountants in the United States who have passed the Uniform _____ Examination and have met additional state education and experience requirements for certification as a _____. Individuals who have passed the Exam but have not either accomplished the required on-the-job experience or have previously met it but in the meantime have lapsed their continuing professional education are, in many states, permitted the designation '_____ Inactive' or an equivalent phrase. In most U.S. states, only _____s who are licensed are able to provide to the public attestation (including auditing) opinions on financial statements.
   a. Certified General Accountant
   b. Chartered Accountant
   c. Chartered Certified Accountant
   d. Certified Public Accountant

42. _____ is the set of processes, customs, policies, laws, and institutions affecting the way a corporation is directed, administered or controlled. _____ also includes the relationships among the many stakeholders involved and the goals for which the corporation is governed. The principal stakeholders are the shareholders/members, management, and the board of directors.
   a. Patent
   b. Corporate governance
   c. Trust indenture
   d. FLSA

43. The _____ of 2002 (Pub.L. 107-204, 116 Stat. 745, enacted July 30, 2002), also known as the Public Company Accounting Reform and Investor Protection Act of 2002, is a United States federal law enacted on July 30, 2002 in response to a number of major corporate and accounting scandals including those affecting Enron, Tyco International, Adelphia, Peregrine Systems and WorldCom. The legislation establishes new or enhanced standards for all U.S. public company boards, management, and public accounting firms. It does not apply to privately held companies.

a. Lease
b. Sarbanes-Oxley Act
c. Fair Labor Standards Act
d. FCPA

44. An _____ is a term used in behavioral economics to describe those types of behaviors that impose costs on a person in the long-run that are not taken into account when making decisions in the present. Classical Economics discourages government from creating legislation that targets internalities, because it is assumed that the consumer takes these personal costs into account when paying for the good that causes the _____. For example, cigarettes should be taxed because of the negative consumption externalities that they impose, such as second-hand smoke, not because the smoker harms him or herself by smoking.

a. Internality
b. Inventory turnover ratio
c. Operating budget
d. Authorised capital

45. In accounting and organizational theory, _____ is defined as a process effected by an organization's structure, work and authority flows, people and management information systems, designed to help the organization accomplish specific goals or objectives. It is a means by which an organization's resources are directed, monitored, and measured. It plays an important role in preventing and detecting fraud and protecting the organization's resources, both physical (e.g., machinery and property) and intangible (e.g., reputation or intellectual property such as trademarks.)

a. Audit risk
b. Internal control
c. Auditor independence
d. Audit committee

46. _____ is the world's largest professional services firm. It was formed in 1998 from a merger between Price Waterhouse and Coopers ' Lybrand, both formed in London.

_____ earned aggregated worldwide revenues of $28 billion for fiscal 2008, and employed over 146,000 people in 150 countries.

a. Serial bonds
b. Daybook
c. Total-factor productivity
d. PricewaterhouseCoopers

Chapter 1. One Managerial Accounting and the Business Environment   15

47. The term _____ usually refers to a company that is permitted to offer its registered securities (stock, bonds, etc.) for sale to the general public, typically through a stock exchange, or occasionally a company whose stock is traded over the counter (OTC) via market makers who use non-exchange quotation services.

The term '_____' may also refer to a company owned by the government.

   a. Governmental Accounting Standards Board
   b. MicroStrategy
   c. Professional association
   d. Public Company

48. The _____ (sometimes called 'Peekaboo') is a private-sector, non-profit corporation created by the Sarbanes-Oxley Act, a 2002 United States federal law, to oversee the auditors of public companies. Its stated purpose is to 'protect the interests of investors and further the public interest in the preparation of informative, fair, and independent audit reports'. Although a private entity, the _____ has many government-like regulatory functions, making it in some ways similar to the private Self Regulatory Organizations (SROs) that regulate stock markets and other aspects of the financial markets in the United States.
   a. Pension Benefit Guaranty Corporation
   b. Public Company Accounting Oversight Board
   c. 3M Company
   d. Financial Crimes Enforcement Network

49. Radio-frequency identification (_____) is the use of an object (typically referred to as an _____ tag) applied to or incorporated into a product, animal, or person for the purpose of identification and tracking using radio waves. Some tags can be read from several meters away and beyond the line of sight of the reader.

Most _____ tags contain at least two parts.

   a. BMC Software, Inc.
   b. BNSF Railway
   c. 3M Company
   d. RFID

Chapter 2. Two Cost Terms, Concepts, and Classifications

1. _____ is the term used to refer to the standard framework of guidelines for financial accounting used in any given jurisdiction. _____ includes the standards, conventions, and rules accountants follow in recording and summarizing transactions, and in the preparation of financial statements.

Financial accounting information must be assembled and reported objectively.

   a. Current asset
   b. Long-term liabilities
   c. General ledger
   d. Generally accepted accounting principles

2. A _____ is something that is acted upon or used by or by human labour or industry, for use as a building material to create some product or structure. Often the term is used to denote material that came from nature and is in an unprocessed or minimally processed state. Iron ore, logs, and crude oil, would be examples.

   a. Raw material
   b. BNSF Railway
   c. 3M Company
   d. BMC Software, Inc.

3. _____ is a costing model that identifies activities in an organization and assigns the cost of each activity resource to all products and services according to the actual consumption by each: it assigns more indirect costs (overhead) into direct costs.

In this way an organization can establish the true cost of its individual products and services for the purposes of identifying and eliminating those which are unprofitable and lowering the prices of those which are overpriced.

In a business organization, the ABC methodology assigns an organization's resource costs through activities to the products and services provided to its customers.

   a. ABC Television Network
   b. Indirect costs
   c. Activity-based costing
   d. Activity-based management

4. In economics, business, retail, and accounting, a _____ is the value of money that has been used up to produce something, and hence is not available for use anymore. In economics, a _____ is an alternative that is given up as a result of a decision. In business, the _____ may be one of acquisition, in which case the amount of money expended to acquire it is counted as _____.

Chapter 2. Two Cost Terms, Concepts, and Classifications   17

   a. Cost of quality
   b. Cost allocation
   c. Prime cost
   d. Cost

5. Project _____: The project _____ is a prediction of the costs associated with a particular company project. These costs include labor, materials, and other related expenses. The project _____ is often broken down into specific tasks, with task _____s assigned to each.

   a. 3M Company
   b. Budget
   c. BNSF Railway
   d. BMC Software, Inc.

6. _____ is the total cost involved in operating all production facilities of a manufacturing business. It generally applies to indirect labor and indirect cost, it also includes all costs involved in manufacturing with the exception of the cost of raw materials and direct labor. _____ also includes certain costs such as quality assurance costs, cleanup costs, and property insurance premiums.

   a. Factory overhead
   b. Profit center
   c. Contribution margin analysis
   d. Cost driver

7. In business, _____, Overhead cost or _____ expense refers to an ongoing expense of operating a business. The term _____ is usually used to group expenses that are necessary to the continued functioning of the business, but do not directly generate profits.

_____ expenses are all costs on the income statement except for direct labor and direct materials.

   a. Intangible assets
   b. ABC Television Network
   c. AIG
   d. Overhead

8. _____ is a cornerstone of accrual accounting together with the revenue recognition principle. They both determine the accounting period, in which revenues and expenses are recognized. According to the principle, expenses are recognized when obligations are (1) incurred (usually when goods are transferred or services rendered, e.g. sold), and (2) offset against recognized revenues, which were generated from those expenses (related on the cause-and-effect basis), no matter when cash is paid out.

Chapter 2. Two Cost Terms, Concepts, and Classifications

a. Matching principle
b. Net sales
c. Payroll
d. Current liabilities

9. Direct labor and overhead are often called conversion cost while direct material and direct labor are often referred to as _____.

For example, a manufacturing firm pays for raw materials. When activity is decreased, less raw material is used, and so the spending for raw materials falls.

a. Cost-volume-profit analysis
b. Marginal cost
c. Prime cost
d. Cost accounting

10. The _____ is a concept from business management that was first described and popularized by Michael Porter in his 1985 best-seller, Competitive Advantage: Creating and Sustaining Superior Performance.

A _____ is a chain of activities. Products pass through all activities of the chain in order and at each activity the product gains some value.

a. Customer relationship management
b. Market segmentation
c. Product differentiation
d. Value chain

11. In financial accounting, a _____ or statement of financial position is a summary of a person's or organization's balances. Assets, liabilities and ownership equity are listed as of a specific date, such as the end of its financial year. A _____ is often described as a snapshot of a company's financial condition.

a. Financial statements
b. 3M Company
c. Statement of retained earnings
d. Balance sheet

12. _____ are formal records of a business' financial activities.

Chapter 2. Two Cost Terms, Concepts, and Classifications   19

In British English, including United Kingdom company law, _____ are often referred to as accounts, although the term _____ is also used, particularly by accountants.

_____ provide an overview of a business' financial condition in both short and long term.

a. Statement of retained earnings
b. 3M Company
c. Notes to the financial statements
d. Financial statements

13. _____s are goods that have completed the manufacturing process but have not yet been sold or distributed to the end user.

Manufacturing has three classes of inventory:

1. Raw material
2. Work in process
3. _____s

A good purchased as a 'raw material' goes into the manufacture of a product. A good only partially completed during the manufacturing process is called 'work in process'. When the good is completed as to manufacturing but not yet sold or distributed to the end-user is called a '_____'.

a. Reorder point
b. FIFO and LIFO accounting
c. 3M Company
d. Finished good

14.   In financial accounting, a _____ or Statement of cash flows is a financial statement that shows a company's flow of cash. The money coming into the business is called cash inflow, and money going out from the business is called cash outflow. The statement shows how changes in balance sheet and income accounts affect cash and cash equivalents, and breaks the analysis down to operating, investing, and financing activities.
a. BMC Software, Inc.
b. 3M Company
c. BNSF Railway
d. Cash flow statement

Chapter 2. Two Cost Terms, Concepts, and Classifications

15. _____ or in-process inventory includes the set at large of unfinished items for products in a production process. These items are not yet completed but either just being fabricated or waiting in a queue for further processing or in a buffer storage. The term is used in production and supply chain management.
   a. BMC Software, Inc.
   b. 3M Company
   c. BNSF Railway
   d. Work in process

16. _____ is the balance of the amounts of cash being received and paid by a business during a defined period of time, sometimes tied to a specific project. Measurement of _____ can be used

   - to evaluate the state or performance of a business or project.
   - to determine problems with liquidity. Being profitable does not necessarily mean being liquid. A company can fail because of a shortage of cash, even while profitable.
   - to project rate of returns. The time of _____s into and out of projects are used as inputs to financial models such as internal rate of return, and net present value.
   - to examine income or growth of a business when it is believed that accrual accounting concepts do not represent economic realities. Alternately, _____ can be used to 'validate' the net income generated by accrual accounting.

   _____ as a generic term may be used differently depending on context, and certain _____ definitions may be adapted by analysts and users for their own uses. Common terms include operating _____ and free _____.

   a. Cash flow
   b. Controlling interest
   c. Commercial paper
   d. Flow-through entity

17. A _____ is a tangible input for a product manufactured/Service provided, like labor or material. For example a cloth manufacturing firm requires some amount of predetermined labor and predetermined raw material for any amount of cloth being manufactured. The cost of employing labor can be directly fixed as 'per man per hour' or 'per man per day', so the labor is a _____ as you can directly associate cost with it.
   a. Residual value
   b. Round-tripping
   c. 3M Company
   d. Cost object

18. _____ is a company's financial statement that indicates how the revenue is transformed into the net income The purpose of the _____ is to show managers and investors whether the company made or lost money during the period being reported.

Chapter 2. Two Cost Terms, Concepts, and Classifications 21

The important thing to remember about an _____ is that it represents a period of time.

a. AMEX
b. AIG
c. ABC Television Network
d. Income statement

19. Total _____ is a method of Accounting cost which entails the full cost of manufacturing or providing a service. This includes not just the costs of materials and labour, but also of all manufacturing overheads (whether e;fixede; or e;variablee;.) One of the main reasons for absorbing overheads into the cost of units is for inventory valuation purposes.

a. AMEX
b. Absorption costing
c. ABC Television Network
d. AIG

20. In economics, _____ are business expenses that are not dependent on the activities of the business They tend to be time-related, such as salaries or rents being paid per month. This is in contrast to variable costs, which are volume-related (and are paid per quantity.)

In management accounting, _____ are defined as expenses that do not change in proportion to the activity of a business, within the relevant period or scale of production.

a. Cost accounting
b. Fixed costs
c. Marginal cost
d. Cost of quality

21. An _____ is a term used in behavioral economics to describe those types of behaviors that impose costs on a person in the long-run that are not taken into account when making decisions in the present. Classical Economics discourages government from creating legislation that targets internalities, because it is assumed that the consumer takes these personal costs into account when paying for the good that causes the _____. For example, cigarettes should be taxed because of the negative consumption externalities that they impose, such as second-hand smoke, not because the smoker harms him or herself by smoking.

a. Inventory turnover ratio
b. Operating budget
c. Authorised capital
d. Internality

Chapter 2. Two Cost Terms, Concepts, and Classifications

22. _____ or economic opportunity loss is the value of the next best alternative foregone as the result of making a decision. _____ analysis is an important part of a company's decision-making processes but is not treated as an actual cost in any financial statement. The next best thing that a person can engage in is referred to as the _____ of doing the best thing and ignoring the next best thing to be done.
   a. Opportunity cost
   b. ABC Television Network
   c. Inflation
   d. AIG

23. _____s are expenses that change in proportion to the activity of a business. In other words, _____ is the sum of marginal costs. It can also be considered normal costs.
   a. Quality costs
   b. Cost accounting
   c. Fixed costs
   d. Variable cost

24. _____ can be regarded as an outcome of mental processes (cognitive process) leading to the selection of a course of action among several alternatives. Every _____ process produces a final choice. The output can be an action or an opinion of choice.
   a. BMC Software, Inc.
   b. BNSF Railway
   c. 3M Company
   d. Decision making

25. In economics and finance, _____ is the change in total cost that arises when the quantity produced changes by one unit. It is the cost of producing one more unit of a good. Mathematically, the _____ function is expressed as the first derivative of the total cost (TC) function with respect to quantity (Q.)
   a. Cost of quality
   b. Marginal cost
   c. Variable cost
   d. Cost accounting

Chapter 2. Two Cost Terms, Concepts, and Classifications

26. _____ is the amount of time someone works beyond normal working hours. Normal hours may be determined in several ways:

- by custom (what is considered healthy or reasonable by society),
- by practices of a given trade or profession,
- by legislation,
- by agreement between employers and workers or their representatives.

Most nations have _____ laws designed to dissuade or prevent employers from forcing their employees to work excessively long hours. These laws may take into account other considerations than the humanitarian, such as increasing the overall level of employment in the economy. One common approach to regulating _____ is to require employers to pay workers at a higher hourly rate for _____ work.

a. AIG
b. AMEX
c. Overtime
d. ABC Television Network

27. In probability theory and statistics, the _____ of a random variable, probability distribution averaging the squared distance of its possible values from the expected value (mean.) Whereas the mean is a way to describe the location of a distribution, the _____ is a way to capture its scale or degree of being spread out. The unit of _____ is the square of the unit of the original variable.

a. Time series
b. Statistics
c. Monte Carlo methods
d. Variance

28. The concept of _____ is a means to quantify the total cost of quality-related efforts and deficiencies. It was first described by Armand V. Feigenbaum in a 1956 Harvard Business Review article.

Prior to its introduction, the general perception was that higher quality requires higher costs, either by buying better materials or machines or by hiring more labor.

a. Quality costs
b. Marginal cost
c. Cost allocation
d. Variable cost

Chapter 2. Two Cost Terms, Concepts, and Classifications

29. _____ and benefits in kind are various non-wage compensations provided to employees in addition to their normal wages or salaries. Where an employee exchanges (cash) wages for some other form of benefit, this is generally referred to as a 'salary sacrifice' arrangement. In most countries, most kinds of _____ are taxable to at least some degree.
    a. AMEX
    b. ABC Television Network
    c. AIG
    d. Employee benefits

30. Just in Time could refer to the following:

    - _____, an inventory strategy that reduces in-process inventory
    - _____ compilation, a technique for improving the performance of bytecode-compiled programming systems

    a. Comparable
    b. Just-in-time
    c. Help desk and incident reporting auditing
    d. Fiscal

31. _____ is an effective method of monitoring a process through the use of control charts. Control charts enable the use of objective criteria for distinguishing background variation from events of significance based on statistical techniques. Much of its power lies in the ability to monitor both process center and its variation about that center.
    a. 3M Company
    b. BMC Software, Inc.
    c. Statistical process control
    d. BNSF Railway

32. An _____ is a practitioner of accountancy, which is the measurement, disclosure or provision of assurance about financial information that helps managers, investors, tax authorities and other decision makers make resource allocation decisions.

The word '_____' is derived from the French 'Compter' which took its origin from the Latin 'Computare'. The word was formerly written in English as 'Accomptant', but in process of time the word, which was always pronounced by dropping the 'p', became gradually changed both in pronunciation and in orthography to its present form.

a. AIG
b. ABC Television Network
c. AMEX
d. Accountant

33. The _____ is the national, professional association of CPAs in the United States, with more than 330,000 members, including CPAs in business and industry, public practice, government, and education; student affiliates; and international associates. It sets ethical standards for the profession and U.S. auditing standards for audits of private companies; federal, state and local governments; and non-profit organizations.

Approximately 40% of its members are engaged in the practice of public accounting, in areas such as auditing, accounting, taxation, general business consulting, business valuation, personal financial planning and business technology.

a. American Institute of Certified Public Accountants
b. ABC Television Network
c. AIG
d. Other postemployment benefits

34. _____ is the statutory title of qualified accountants in the United States who have passed the Uniform _____ Examination and have met additional state education and experience requirements for certification as a _____. Individuals who have passed the Exam but have not either accomplished the required on-the-job experience or have previously met it but in the meantime have lapsed their continuing professional education are, in many states, permitted the designation '_____ Inactive' or an equivalent phrase. In most U.S. states, only _____s who are licensed are able to provide to the public attestation (including auditing) opinions on financial statements.

a. Chartered Certified Accountant
b. Certified General Accountant
c. Chartered Accountant
d. Certified Public Accountant

35. The International Organization for Standardization (Organisation internationale de normalisation), widely known as _____, is an international-standard-setting body composed of representatives from various national standards organizations. Founded on 23 February 1947, the organization promulgates worldwide proprietary industrial and commercial standards. It is headquartered in Geneva, Switzerland.

a. AMEX
b. AIG
c. ABC Television Network
d. ISO

36. The _____, widely known as ISO , is an international-standard-setting body composed of representatives from various national standards organizations. Founded on 23 February 1947, the organization promulgates worldwide proprietary industrial and commercial standards. It is headquartered in Geneva, Switzerland.

  a. ABC Television Network
  b. AIG
  c. AMEX
  d. International Organization for Standardization

37. _____ is a business management strategy, initially implemented by Motorola, that today enjoys widespread application in many sectors of industry.

_____ seeks to improve the quality of process outputs by identifying and removing the causes of defects (errors) and variation in manufacturing and business processes. It uses a set of quality management methods, including statistical methods, and creates a special infrastructure of people within the organization ('Black Belts' etc.)

  a. Six Sigma
  b. Theory of constraints
  c. Lean manufacturing
  d. Make to order

Chapter 3. Three Systems Design: Job-Order Costing

1. The title _____ is a professional designation awarded by various professional bodies around the world.

    The _____ designation is a post-nominal award issued to individuals who have achieved a peer-based criteria of professional competency in the field of Management Accounting. Management accounting qualifications differ from those such as the ACA or CPA 'Chartered' or 'Public' accounting qualifications in a number of ways.

    a. BMC Software, Inc.
    b. 3M Company
    c. Convey Compliance Systems
    d. Certified management accountant

2. In cost-volume-profit analysis, a form of management accounting, _____ is the marginal profit per unit sale. It is a useful quantity in carrying out various calculations, and can be used as a measure of operating leverage.

    The Total _____ is Total Revenue (TR, or Sales) minus Total Variable Cost (TVC):

    Tcontribution margin = TR − TVC

    The Unit _____ (C) is Unit Revenue (Price, P) minus Unit Variable Cost (V):

    C = P − V

    The _____ Ratio is the percentage of Contribution over Total Revenue, which can be calculated from the unit contribution over unit price or total contribution over Total Revenue:

    $$\frac{C}{P} = \frac{P-V}{P} = \frac{\text{Unit Contribution Margin}}{\text{Price}} = \frac{\text{Total Contribution Margin}}{\text{Total Revenue}}$$

    For instance, if the price is $10 and the unit variable cost is $2, then the unit _____ is $8, and the _____ ratio is $8/$10 = 80%.

    a. Factory overhead
    b. Cost management
    c. Profit center
    d. Contribution margin

3. _____ is an accounting methodology that traces and accumulates direct costs, and allocates indirect costs of a manufacturing process. Costs are assigned to products, usually in a large batch, which might include an entire month's production. Eventually, costs have to be allocated to individual units of product.

a. Process costing
b. Profit center
c. Cost driver
d. Cost management

4. Total _____ is a method of Accounting cost which entails the full cost of manufacturing or providing a service. This includes not just the costs of materials and labour, but also of all manufacturing overheads (whether e;fixede; or e;variablee;.) One of the main reasons for absorbing overheads into the cost of units is for inventory valuation purposes.
   a. AMEX
   b. AIG
   c. ABC Television Network
   d. Absorption costing

5. An _____ is a practitioner of accountancy, which is the measurement, disclosure or provision of assurance about financial information that helps managers, investors, tax authorities and other decision makers make resource allocation decisions.

The word '_____' is derived from the French 'Compter' which took its origin from the Latin 'Computare'. The word was formerly written in English as 'Accomptant', but in process of time the word, which was always pronounced by dropping the 'p', became gradually changed both in pronunciation and in orthography to its present form.

   a. AMEX
   b. ABC Television Network
   c. AIG
   d. Accountant

6. In economics, business, retail, and accounting, a _____ is the value of money that has been used up to produce something, and hence is not available for use anymore. In economics, a _____ is an alternative that is given up as a result of a decision. In business, the _____ may be one of acquisition, in which case the amount of money expended to acquire it is counted as _____.
   a. Prime cost
   b. Cost of quality
   c. Cost allocation
   d. Cost

Chapter 3. Three Systems Design: Job-Order Costing

7. _____ is concerned with the provisions and use of accounting information to managers within organizations, to provide them with the basis to make informed business decisions that will allow them to be better equipped in their management and control functions.

In contrast to financial accountancy information, _____ information is:

- usually confidential and used by management, instead of publicly reported;
- forward-looking, instead of historical;
- pragmatically computed using extensive management information systems and internal controls, instead of complying with accounting standards.

This is because of the different emphasis: _____ information is used within an organization, typically for decision-making.

a. Grenzplankostenrechnung
b. Nonassurance services
c. Governmental accounting
d. Management accounting

8. In business, _____, Overhead cost or _____ expense refers to an ongoing expense of operating a business. The term _____ is usually used to group expenses that are necessary to the continued functioning of the business, but do not directly generate profits.

_____ expenses are all costs on the income statement except for direct labor and direct materials.

a. AIG
b. ABC Television Network
c. Intangible assets
d. Overhead

9. _____ is a list of the raw materials, sub-assemblies, intermediate assemblies, sub-components, components, parts and the quantities of each needed to manufacture an end item (final product).
a. Bill of materials
b. Changeover
c. Deming Prize
d. Cellular manufacturing

10. A _____ is the rate used to apply manufacturing overhead to work-in-process inventory. It is calculated as estimated manufacturing overhead cost divided by estimated amount of cost driver or activity base. Common activity bases used in the calculation include direct labor costs, direct labor hours, or machine hours.

a. Sensitivity analysis
b. Kaizen
c. Procurement
d. Pre-determined overhead rate

11. A '_____' is the unit of an activity that causes the change of an activity cost. A _____ is any activity that causes a cost to be incurred. The Activity Based Costing (ABC) approach relates indirect cost to the activities that drive them to be incurred.
   a. Profit center
   b. Factory overhead
   c. Cost driver
   d. Contribution margin analysis

12. _____ is a process of attributing cost to particular cost centres. For example the wage of the driver of the purchasing department can be allocated to the purchasing department cost centre. It is not necessary to share the wage cost over several different cost centers.
   a. Cost accounting
   b. Cost allocation
   c. Cost of quality
   d. Variable cost

13. _____ is a costing model that identifies activities in an organization and assigns the cost of each activity resource to all products and services according to the actual consumption by each: it assigns more indirect costs (overhead) into direct costs.

In this way an organization can establish the true cost of its individual products and services for the purposes of identifying and eliminating those which are unprofitable and lowering the prices of those which are overpriced.

In a business organization, the ABC methodology assigns an organization's resource costs through activities to the products and services provided to its customers.

   a. Activity-based costing
   b. Activity-based management
   c. Indirect costs
   d. ABC Television Network

Chapter 3. Three Systems Design: Job-Order Costing

14. A _____ is something that is acted upon or used by or by human labour or industry, for use as a building material to create some product or structure. Often the term is used to denote material that came from nature and is in an unprocessed or minimally processed state. Iron ore, logs, and crude oil, would be examples.
   a. 3M Company
   b. BNSF Railway
   c. BMC Software, Inc.
   d. Raw material

15. A _____ is the pinnacle activity involved in selling products or services in return for money or other compensation. It is an act of completion of a commercial activity.

A _____ is completed by the seller, the owner of the goods.

   a. Maturity
   b. High yield stock
   c. Tertiary sector of economy
   d. Sale

16. A _____ is usually a temporary account containing costs or amounts that are to be transferred to another account. An example is the income summary account containing revenue and expense amounts to be transferred to retained earnings at the close of a fiscal period.
   a. Special assessment
   b. Clearing account
   c. Tax Analysts
   d. Fixed tax

17. In financial accounting, _____ or cost of sales includes the direct costs attributable to the production of the goods sold by a company. This amount includes the materials cost used in creating the goods along with the direct labor costs used to produce the good. It excludes indirect expenses such as distribution costs and sales force costs.
   a. Reorder point
   b. 3M Company
   c. FIFO and LIFO accounting
   d. Cost of goods sold

18. A _____ is a habit, a preparation, a state of readiness, or a tendency to act in a specified way.

The terms dispositional belief and occurrent belief refer, in the former case, to a belief that is held in the mind but not currently being considered, and in the latter case, to a belief that is currently being considered by the mind.

In Bourdieu's theory of fields _____s are the natural tendencies of each individual to take on a certain position in any field.

a. Disposition
b. BNSF Railway
c. 3M Company
d. BMC Software, Inc.

19. In economics, _____ is the ratio of the percent change in one variable to the percent change in another variable. It is a tool for measuring the responsiveness of a function to changes in parameters in a relative way. Commonly analyzed are _____ of substitution, price and wealth.
a. Elasticity
b. U-Haul
c. Economic value added
d. Old Navy

20. _____ is the difference between the cost of a good or service and its selling price. A _____ is added on to the total cost incurred by the producer of a good or service in order to create a profit. The total cost reflects the total amount of both fixed and variable expenses to produce and distribute a product.
a. Corporate Bond
b. Markup
c. Statements of Financial Accounting Standards No. 133, Accounting for Derivative Instruments and Hedging Activities
d. Merck ' Co., Inc.

21. Procter is a surname, and may also refer to:

- Bryan Waller Procter (pseud. Barry Cornwall), English poet
- Goodwin Procter, American law firm
- _____, consumer products multinational

a. Screening
b. Markup
c. Welfare
d. Procter ' Gamble

Chapter 4. Four Systems Design: Process Costing

1. Procter is a surname, and may also refer to:

   - Bryan Waller Procter (pseud. Barry Cornwall), English poet
   - Goodwin Procter, American law firm
   - _____, consumer products multinational

   a. Screening
   b. Welfare
   c. Markup
   d. Procter ' Gamble

2. _____ is an acronym for First In, First Out, an abstraction in ways of organizing and manipulation of data relative to time and prioritization. This expression describes the principle of a queue processing technique or servicing conflicting demands by ordering process by first-come, first-served (FCFS) behaviour: what comes in first is handled first, what comes in next waits until the first is finished, etc.

   Thus it is analogous to the behaviour of persons queueing (or 'standing in line', in common American parlance), where the persons leave the queue in the order they arrive, or waiting one's turn at a traffic control signal.

   a. Trademark
   b. Kanban
   c. Risk management
   d. FIFO

3. In economics, business, retail, and accounting, a _____ is the value of money that has been used up to produce something, and hence is not available for use anymore. In economics, a _____ is an alternative that is given up as a result of a decision. In business, the _____ may be one of acquisition, in which case the amount of money expended to acquire it is counted as _____.
   a. Cost allocation
   b. Cost
   c. Prime cost
   d. Cost of quality

4. In business, _____, Overhead cost or _____ expense refers to an ongoing expense of operating a business. The term _____ is usually used to group expenses that are necessary to the continued functioning of the business, but do not directly generate profits.

   _____ expenses are all costs on the income statement except for direct labor and direct materials.

Chapter 4. Four Systems Design: Process Costing

  a. ABC Television Network
  b. AIG
  c. Intangible assets
  d. Overhead

5. _____ is an accounting methodology that traces and accumulates direct costs, and allocates indirect costs of a manufacturing process. Costs are assigned to products, usually in a large batch, which might include an entire month's production. Eventually, costs have to be allocated to individual units of product.

  a. Cost driver
  b. Profit center
  c. Cost management
  d. Process costing

6. The title _____ is a professional designation awarded by various professional bodies around the world.

The _____ designation is a post-nominal award issued to individuals who have achieved a peer-based criteria of professional competency in the field of Management Accounting. Management accounting qualifications differ from those such as the ACA or CPA 'Chartered' or 'Public' accounting qualifications in a number of ways.

  a. Convey Compliance Systems
  b. Certified management accountant
  c. BMC Software, Inc.
  d. 3M Company

7. In cost-volume-profit analysis, a form of management accounting, _____ is the marginal profit per unit sale. It is a useful quantity in carrying out various calculations, and can be used as a measure of operating leverage.

The Total _____ is Total Revenue (TR, or Sales) minus Total Variable Cost (TVC):

  Tcontribution margin = TR − TVC

The Unit _____ (C) is Unit Revenue (Price, P) minus Unit Variable Cost (V):

  C = P − V

The _____ Ratio is the percentage of Contribution over Total Revenue, which can be calculated from the unit contribution over unit price or total contribution over Total Revenue:

$$\frac{C}{P} = \frac{P-V}{P} = \frac{\text{Unit Contribution Margin}}{\text{Price}} = \frac{\text{Total Contribution Margin}}{\text{Total Revenue}}$$

For instance, if the price is $10 and the unit variable cost is $2, then the unit _____ is $8, and the _____ ratio is $8/$10 = 80%.

a. Profit center
b. Cost management
c. Factory overhead
d. Contribution margin

8. The term _____, derived from the distinctive T shape, is frequently used when discussing or analyzing accounting or business transactions. _____s are used to represent general ledger accounts.

Typically one or more Ts are drawn on a white board or blank piece of paper. A general ledger account name or number is then written above each T. Debit entries are recorded on the left side of the 'T' and credit entries are recorded on the right side of the 'T'.

a. 3M Company
b. T account
c. BNSF Railway
d. BMC Software, Inc.

9. An _____ is a practitioner of accountancy, which is the measurement, disclosure or provision of assurance about financial information that helps managers, investors, tax authorities and other decision makers make resource allocation decisions.

The word '_____' is derived from the French 'Compter' which took its origin from the Latin 'Computare'. The word was formerly written in English as 'Accomptant', but in process of time the word, which was always pronounced by dropping the 'p', became gradually changed both in pronunciation and in orthography to its present form.

a. AIG
b. ABC Television Network
c. AMEX
d. Accountant

10. _____ is concerned with the provisions and use of accounting information to managers within organizations, to provide them with the basis to make informed business decisions that will allow them to be better equipped in their management and control functions.

In contrast to financial accountancy information, _____ information is:

- usually confidential and used by management, instead of publicly reported;
- forward-looking, instead of historical;
- pragmatically computed using extensive management information systems and internal controls, instead of complying with accounting standards.

This is because of the different emphasis: _____ information is used within an organization, typically for decision-making.

a. Grenzplankostenrechnung
b. Governmental accounting
c. Nonassurance services
d. Management accounting

11. _____ is a process of attributing cost to particular cost centres. For example the wage of the driver of the purchasing department can be allocated to the purchasing department cost centre. It is not necessary to share the wage cost over several different cost centers.
a. Cost of quality
b. Cost allocation
c. Variable cost
d. Cost accounting

12. The concept of quality costs is a means to quantify the total _____-related efforts and deficiencies. It was first described by Armand V. Feigenbaum in a 1956 Harvard Business Review article.

Prior to its introduction, the general perception was that higher quality requires higher costs, either by buying better materials or machines or by hiring more labor.

Chapter 4. Four Systems Design: Process Costing

a. Marginal cost
b. Cost of quality
c. Cost accounting
d. Quality costs

13. The concept of _____ is a means to quantify the total cost of quality-related efforts and deficiencies. It was first described by Armand V. Feigenbaum in a 1956 Harvard Business Review article.

Prior to its introduction, the general perception was that higher quality requires higher costs, either by buying better materials or machines or by hiring more labor.

a. Quality costs
b. Marginal cost
c. Variable cost
d. Cost allocation

14. _____, in law and economics, is a form of risk management primarily used to hedge against the risk of a contingent loss. _____ is defined as the equitable transfer of the risk of a loss, from one entity to another, in exchange for a premium, and can be thought of as a guaranteed small loss to prevent a large, possibly devastating loss. An insurer is a company selling the _____; an insured is the person or entity buying the _____.

a. Insurance
b. ABC Television Network
c. AMEX
d. AIG

15. Total _____ is a method of Accounting cost which entails the full cost of manufacturing or providing a service. This includes not just the costs of materials and labour, but also of all manufacturing overheads (whether e;fixede; or e;variablee;.) One of the main reasons for absorbing overheads into the cost of units is for inventory valuation purposes.

a. Absorption costing
b. ABC Television Network
c. AIG
d. AMEX

Chapter 5. Five Cost Behavior: Analysis and Use

1. In economics, business, retail, and accounting, a _____ is the value of money that has been used up to produce something, and hence is not available for use anymore. In economics, a _____ is an alternative that is given up as a result of a decision. In business, the _____ may be one of acquisition, in which case the amount of money expended to acquire it is counted as _____.
   a. Cost allocation
   b. Cost
   c. Prime cost
   d. Cost of quality

2. In economics, _____ are business expenses that are not dependent on the activities of the business They tend to be time-related, such as salaries or rents being paid per month. This is in contrast to variable costs, which are volume-related (and are paid per quantity.)

   In management accounting, _____ are defined as expenses that do not change in proportion to the activity of a business, within the relevant period or scale of production.

   a. Marginal cost
   b. Cost of quality
   c. Cost accounting
   d. Fixed costs

3. _____s are expenses that change in proportion to the activity of a business. In other words, _____ is the sum of marginal costs. It can also be considered normal costs.
   a. Cost accounting
   b. Variable cost
   c. Quality costs
   d. Fixed costs

4. A '_____' is the unit of an activity that causes the change of an activity cost. A _____ is any activity that causes a cost to be incurred. The Activity Based Costing (ABC) approach relates indirect cost to the activities that drive them to be incurred.
   a. Contribution margin analysis
   b. Profit center
   c. Factory overhead
   d. Cost driver

Chapter 5. Five Cost Behavior: Analysis and Use

5. _____, commonly known as e-commerce or eCommerce, consists of the buying and selling of products or services over electronic systems such as the Internet and other computer networks. The amount of trade conducted electronically has grown extraordinarily since the spread of the Internet. A wide variety of commerce is conducted in this way, spurring and drawing on innovations in electronic funds transfer, supply chain management, Internet marketing, online transaction processing, electronic data interchange (EDI), inventory management systems, and automated data collection systems.

   a. AIG
   b. ABC Television Network
   c. Electronic data interchange
   d. Electronic commerce

6. _____ is an open standard which supports information modeling and the expression of semantic meaning commonly required in business reporting. _____ is XML-based. It uses the XML syntax and related XML technologies such as XML Schema, XLink, XPath, and Namespaces to articulate this semantic meaning. One use of _____ is to define and exchange financial information, such as a financial statement.

   a. BNSF Railway
   b. XBRL
   c. 3M Company
   d. BMC Software, Inc.

7. _____ is subcontracting a process, such as product design or manufacturing, to a third-party company. The decision to outsource is often made in the interest of lowering cost or making better use of time and energy costs, redirecting or conserving energy directed at the competencies of a particular business, or to make more efficient use of land, labor, capital, (information) technology and resources. _____ became part of the business lexicon during the 1980s.

   a. Outsourcing
   b. Economic Growth and Tax Relief Reconciliation Act of 2001
   c. US Airways, Inc.
   d. USA Today

8. A _____ is a compensation, usually financial, received by a worker in exchange for their labor.

Compensation in terms of _____s is given to worker and compensation in terms of salary is given to employees. Compensation is a monetary benefits given to employees in returns of the services provided by them.

   a. Retirement plan
   b. 3M Company
   c. BMC Software, Inc.
   d. Wage

Chapter 5. Five Cost Behavior: Analysis and Use

9. Project _____: The project _____ is a prediction of the costs associated with a particular company project. These costs include labor, materials, and other related expenses. The project _____ is often broken down into specific tasks, with task _____s assigned to each.
   a. BNSF Railway
   b. BMC Software, Inc.
   c. Budget
   d. 3M Company

10. A _____ is a form of periodic payment from an employer to an employee, which may be specified in an employment contract. It is contrasted with piece wages, where each job, hour or other unit is paid separately, rather than on a periodic basis.

   From the point of a view of running a business, _____ can also be viewed as the cost of acquiring human resources for running operations, and is then termed personnel expense or _____ expense.

   a. BMC Software, Inc.
   b. 3M Company
   c. Separation of duties
   d. Salary

11. The term '_____' refers to the concept of collecting information and attempting to spot a pattern in the information. In some fields of study, the term '_____' has more formally-defined meanings.

   In project management _____ is a mathematical technique that uses historical results to predict future outcome.

   a. Regression analysis
   b. Multicollinearity
   c. Trend analysis
   d. 3M Company

12. The terms '_____' and 'independent variable' are used in similar but subtly different ways in mathematics and statistics as part of the standard terminology in those subjects. They are used to distinguish between two types of quantities being considered, separating them into those available at the start of a process and those being created by it, where the latter (_____s) are dependent on the former (independent variables.)

   In traditional calculus, a function is defined as a relation between two terms called variables because their values vary.

a. BMC Software, Inc.
b. 3M Company
c. Dependent variable
d. BNSF Railway

13. The terms 'dependent variable' and '_____' are used in similar but subtly different ways in mathematics and statistics as part of the standard terminology in those subjects. They are used to distinguish between two types of quantities being considered, separating them into those available at the start of a process and those being created by it, where the latter (dependent variables) are dependent on the former (_____s.)

In traditional calculus, a function is defined as a relation between two terms called variables because their values vary.

a. AMEX
b. ABC Television Network
c. AIG
d. Independent variable

14. _____ is a common concept in economics, and gives rise to derived concepts such as consumer debt. Generally _____ is defined by opposition to production. But the precise definition can vary because different schools of economists define production quite differently.

a. Yield
b. Starving the beast
c. Mitigating Control
d. Consumption

15. _____ is a company's financial statement that indicates how the revenue is transformed into the net income The purpose of the _____ is to show managers and investors whether the company made or lost money during the period being reported.

The important thing to remember about an _____ is that it represents a period of time.

a. AIG
b. AMEX
c. ABC Television Network
d. Income statement

Chapter 6. Six Cost-Volume-Profit Relationships

1. _____, in managerial economics is a form of cost accounting. It is a simplified model, useful for elementary instruction and for short-run decisions.

Cost-volume-profit (CVP) analysis expands the use of information provided by breakeven analysis.

   a. Cost-volume-profit analysis
   b. Fixed costs
   c. Cost of quality
   d. Cost accounting

2. Total _____ is a method of Accounting cost which entails the full cost of manufacturing or providing a service. This includes not just the costs of materials and labour, but also of all manufacturing overheads (whether e;fixede; or e;variablee;.) One of the main reasons for absorbing overheads into the cost of units is for inventory valuation purposes.
   a. Absorption costing
   b. AMEX
   c. AIG
   d. ABC Television Network

3. In cost-volume-profit analysis, a form of management accounting, _____ is the marginal profit per unit sale. It is a useful quantity in carrying out various calculations, and can be used as a measure of operating leverage.

The Total _____ is Total Revenue (TR, or Sales) minus Total Variable Cost (TVC):

   Tcontribution margin = TR − TVC

The Unit _____ (C) is Unit Revenue (Price, P) minus Unit Variable Cost (V):

   C = P − V

The _____ Ratio is the percentage of Contribution over Total Revenue, which can be calculated from the unit contribution over unit price or total contribution over Total Revenue:

$$\frac{C}{P} = \frac{P - V}{P} = \frac{\text{Unit Contribution Margin}}{\text{Price}} = \frac{\text{Total Contribution Margin}}{\text{Total Revenue}}$$

For instance, if the price is $10 and the unit variable cost is $2, then the unit _____ is $8, and the _____ ratio is $8/$10 = 80%.

Chapter 6. Six Cost-Volume-Profit Relationships

a. Factory overhead
b. Profit center
c. Contribution margin
d. Cost management

4. In economics ' business, specifically cost accounting, the _____ is the point at which cost or expenses and revenue are equal: there is no net loss or gain, and one has 'broken even'. A profit or a loss has not been made, although opportunity costs have been paid, and capital has received the risk-adjusted, expected return.

For example, if the business sells less than 200 tables each month, it will make a loss, if it sells more, it will be a profit.

a. 3M Company
b. BMC Software, Inc.
c. Defined benefit pension plan
d. Break-even point

5. In economics, _____ are business expenses that are not dependent on the activities of the business They tend to be time-related, such as salaries or rents being paid per month. This is in contrast to variable costs, which are volume-related (and are paid per quantity.)

In management accounting, _____ are defined as expenses that do not change in proportion to the activity of a business, within the relevant period or scale of production.

a. Marginal cost
b. Cost of quality
c. Cost accounting
d. Fixed costs

6. In economics, business, retail, and accounting, a _____ is the value of money that has been used up to produce something, and hence is not available for use anymore. In economics, a _____ is an alternative that is given up as a result of a decision. In business, the _____ may be one of acquisition, in which case the amount of money expended to acquire it is counted as _____.

a. Cost of quality
b. Cost allocation
c. Prime cost
d. Cost

Chapter 6. Six Cost-Volume-Profit Relationships

7. _____ in economics and business is the result of an exchange and from that trade we assign a numerical monetary value to a good, service or asset. If Alice trades Bob 4 apples for an orange, the _____ of an orange is 4 apples. Inversely, the _____ of an apple is 1/4 oranges.
   a. Discounts and allowances
   b. Price
   c. Price discrimination
   d. Transactional Net Margin Method

8. A _____ is the pinnacle activity involved in selling products or services in return for money or other compensation. It is an act of completion of a commercial activity.

   A _____ is completed by the seller, the owner of the goods.

   a. Tertiary sector of economy
   b. Maturity
   c. High yield stock
   d. Sale

9. _____s are expenses that change in proportion to the activity of a business. In other words, _____ is the sum of marginal costs. It can also be considered normal costs.
   a. Cost accounting
   b. Fixed costs
   c. Quality costs
   d. Variable cost

10. Transport or _____ is the movement of people and goods from one location to another. Transport is performed by various modes, such as air, rail, road, water, cable, pipeline and space. The field can be divided into infrastructure, vehicles, and operations.
    a. BNSF Railway
    b. 3M Company
    c. BMC Software, Inc.
    d. Transportation

11. In accounting, _____ has a very specific meaning. It is an outflow of cash or other valuable assets from a person or company to another person or company. This outflow of cash is generally one side of a trade for products or services that have equal or better current or future value to the buyer than to the seller.

Chapter 6. Six Cost-Volume-Profit Relationships 45

a. AIG
b. ABC Television Network
c. AMEX
d. Expense

12. The _____ of a stock or asset fund is the total percentage of fund assets used for administrative, management, advertising (12b-1), and all other expenses. An _____ of 1% per annum means that each year 1% of the fund's total assets will be used to cover expenses. The _____ does not include sales loads or brokerage commissions.
   a. Expense ratio
   b. AMEX
   c. ABC Television Network
   d. AIG

13. _____, commonly known as e-commerce or eCommerce, consists of the buying and selling of products or services over electronic systems such as the Internet and other computer networks. The amount of trade conducted electronically has grown extraordinarily since the spread of the Internet. A wide variety of commerce is conducted in this way, spurring and drawing on innovations in electronic funds transfer, supply chain management, Internet marketing, online transaction processing, electronic data interchange (EDI), inventory management systems, and automated data collection systems.
   a. AIG
   b. Electronic commerce
   c. Electronic data interchange
   d. ABC Television Network

14. The _____ is a measure of how revenue growth translates into growth in operating income. It is a measure of leverage, and of how risky (volatile) a company's operating income is.

There are various measures of _____, which can be interpreted analogously to financial leverage.

   a. Information ratio
   b. AlphaIC
   c. Upside potential ratio
   d. Operating leverage

Chapter 7. Seven Variable Costing: A Tool for Management

1. In economics, business, retail, and accounting, a _____ is the value of money that has been used up to produce something, and hence is not available for use anymore. In economics, a _____ is an alternative that is given up as a result of a decision. In business, the _____ may be one of acquisition, in which case the amount of money expended to acquire it is counted as _____.
   a. Prime cost
   b. Cost of quality
   c. Cost
   d. Cost allocation

2. _____ accounting (Full costA) generally refers to the process of collecting and presenting information (costs as well as advantages) for each proposed alternative when a decision is necessary. A synonym, true cost accounting (TCA) is also often used. Experts consider both terms problematic as definitions of 'true' and 'full' are inherently subjective
   a. Full cost
   b. 3M Company
   c. BNSF Railway
   d. BMC Software, Inc.

3. In accounting, _____ has a very specific meaning. It is an outflow of cash or other valuable assets from a person or company to another person or company. This outflow of cash is generally one side of a trade for products or services that have equal or better current or future value to the buyer than to the seller.
   a. AMEX
   b. AIG
   c. ABC Television Network
   d. Expense

4. Total _____ is a method of Accounting cost which entails the full cost of manufacturing or providing a service. This includes not just the costs of materials and labour, but also of all manufacturing overheads (whether e;fixede; or e;variablee;.) One of the main reasons for absorbing overheads into the cost of units is for inventory valuation purposes.
   a. Absorption costing
   b. ABC Television Network
   c. AMEX
   d. AIG

5. _____ is a company's financial statement that indicates how the revenue is transformed into the net income The purpose of the _____ is to show managers and investors whether the company made or lost money during the period being reported.

The important thing to remember about an _____ is that it represents a period of time.

Chapter 7. Seven Variable Costing: A Tool for Management

a. ABC Television Network
b. AIG
c. AMEX
d. Income statement

6. _____, in accrual accounting, is any account where the asset or liability is not realized until a future date (accounting period), e.g. annuities, charges, taxes, income, etc. The _____ item may be carried, dependent on type of deferral, as either an asset or liability.

a. Cash basis accounting
b. Payroll
c. Pro forma
d. Deferred

7. In business, _____, Overhead cost or _____ expense refers to an ongoing expense of operating a business. The term _____ is usually used to group expenses that are necessary to the continued functioning of the business, but do not directly generate profits.

_____ expenses are all costs on the income statement except for direct labor and direct materials.

a. AIG
b. Overhead
c. Intangible assets
d. ABC Television Network

8. In financial and business accounting, _____ is a measure of a firm's profitability that excludes interest and income tax expenses.

EBIT = Operating Revenue - Operating Expenses (OPEX) + Non-operating Income

Operating Income = Operating Revenue - Operating Expenses

Operating income is the difference between operating revenues and operating expenses, but it is also sometimes used as a synonym for EBIT and operating profit. This is true if the firm has no non-operating income.

a. AMEX
b. ABC Television Network
c. Earnings before interest and taxes
d. AIG

Chapter 7. Seven Variable Costing: A Tool for Management

9. A _____ is a fungible, negotiable instrument representing financial value. they are broadly categorized into debt securities (such as banknotes, bonds and debentures), and equity securities; e.g., common stocks. The company or other entity issuing the _____ is called the issuer.
   a. BMC Software, Inc.
   b. 3M Company
   c. Tracking stock
   d. Security

10. _____ is the difference between operating revenues and operating expenses, but it is also sometimes used as a synonym for EBIT and operating profit. This is true if the firm has no non-_____.

A professional investor contemplating a change to the capital structure of a firm first evaluates a firm's fundamental earnings potential (reflected by Earnings Before Interest, Taxes, Depreciation and Amortization EBITDA and EBIT), and then determines the optimal use of debt vs. equity.

   a. AIG
   b. AMEX
   c. ABC Television Network
   d. Operating income

11. _____, in managerial economics is a form of cost accounting. It is a simplified model, useful for elementary instruction and for short-run decisions.

Cost-volume-profit (CVP) analysis expands the use of information provided by breakeven analysis.

   a. Cost-volume-profit analysis
   b. Cost accounting
   c. Cost of quality
   d. Fixed costs

12. _____ can be regarded as an outcome of mental processes (cognitive process) leading to the selection of a course of action among several alternatives. Every _____ process produces a final choice. The output can be an action or an opinion of choice.
   a. 3M Company
   b. BMC Software, Inc.
   c. BNSF Railway
   d. Decision making

Chapter 7. Seven Variable Costing: A Tool for Management

13. An _____ is a tax levied on the financial income of people, corporations, or other legal entities. Various _____ systems exist, with varying degrees of tax incidence. Income taxation can be progressive, proportional, or regressive.
    a. Ordinary income
    b. Implied level of government service
    c. Individual Retirement Arrangement
    d. Income tax

14. _____ is a costing model that identifies activities in an organization and assigns the cost of each activity resource to all products and services according to the actual consumption by each: it assigns more indirect costs (overhead) into direct costs.

    In this way an organization can establish the true cost of its individual products and services for the purposes of identifying and eliminating those which are unprofitable and lowering the prices of those which are overpriced.

    In a business organization, the ABC methodology assigns an organization's resource costs through activities to the products and services provided to its customers.

    a. Indirect costs
    b. Activity-based costing
    c. Activity-based management
    d. ABC Television Network

15. In economics, _____ or _____ goods or real _____ refers to factors of production used to create goods or services that are not themselves significantly consumed (though they may depreciate) in the production process. _____ goods may be acquired with money or financial _____. In finance and accounting, _____ generally refers to financial wealth, especially that used to start or maintain a business.
    a. Disclosure
    b. Screening
    c. Vyborg Appeal
    d. Capital

16. _____ is the planning process used to determine whether a firm's long term investments such as new machinery, replacement machinery, new plants, new products, and research development projects are worth pursuing. It is budget for major capital, or investment, expenditures.

Many formal methods are used in _____, including the techniques such as

- Net present value
- Profitability index
- Internal rate of return
- Modified Internal Rate of Return
- Equivalent annuity

These methods use the incremental cash flows from each potential investment, or project. Techniques based on accounting earnings and accounting rules are sometimes used - though economists consider this to be improper - such as the accounting rate of return, and 'return on investment.' Simplified and hybrid methods are used as well, such as payback period and discounted payback period.

a. Preferred stock
b. Gross profit
c. Cash flow
d. Capital budgeting

17. _____ is an overall management philosophy introduced by Dr. Eliyahu M. Goldratt in his 1984 book titled The Goal, that is geared to help organizations continually achieve their goal. The title comes from the contention that any manageable system is limited in achieving more of its goal by a very small number of constraints, and that there is always at least one constraint. The _____ process seeks to identify the constraint and restructure the rest of the organization around it, through the use of the Five Focusing Steps.
a. Theory of Constraints
b. Lean production
c. Six Sigma
d. Lean manufacturing

18. Project _____: The project _____ is a prediction of the costs associated with a particular company project. These costs include labor, materials, and other related expenses. The project _____ is often broken down into specific tasks, with task _____s assigned to each.
a. Budget
b. 3M Company
c. BNSF Railway
d. BMC Software, Inc.

19. Lean manufacturing or _____, which is often known simply as 'Lean', is a production practice that considers the expenditure of resources for any goal other than the creation of value for the end customer to be wasteful, and thus a target for elimination. Working from the perspective of the customer who consumes a product or service, 'value' is defined as any action or process that a customer would be willing to pay for. Basically, lean is centered around creating more value with less work.
   a. Six Sigma
   b. Lean manufacturing
   c. Make to order
   d. Lean production

Chapter 8. Eight Activity-Based Costing: A Tool to Aid Decision Making

1. _____ is a costing model that identifies activities in an organization and assigns the cost of each activity resource to all products and services according to the actual consumption by each: it assigns more indirect costs (overhead) into direct costs.

In this way an organization can establish the true cost of its individual products and services for the purposes of identifying and eliminating those which are unprofitable and lowering the prices of those which are overpriced.

In a business organization, the ABC methodology assigns an organization's resource costs through activities to the products and services provided to its customers.

   a. Activity-based management
   b. Indirect costs
   c. ABC Television Network
   d. Activity-based costing

2. In economics, business, retail, and accounting, a _____ is the value of money that has been used up to produce something, and hence is not available for use anymore. In economics, a _____ is an alternative that is given up as a result of a decision. In business, the _____ may be one of acquisition, in which case the amount of money expended to acquire it is counted as _____.
   a. Prime cost
   b. Cost allocation
   c. Cost of quality
   d. Cost

3. In business, _____, Overhead cost or _____ expense refers to an ongoing expense of operating a business. The term _____ is usually used to group expenses that are necessary to the continued functioning of the business, but do not directly generate profits.

_____ expenses are all costs on the income statement except for direct labor and direct materials.

   a. Overhead
   b. Intangible assets
   c. ABC Television Network
   d. AIG

4. A '_____' is the unit of an activity that causes the change of an activity cost. A _____ is any activity that causes a cost to be incurred. The Activity Based Costing (ABC) approach relates indirect cost to the activities that drive them to be incurred.

Chapter 8. Eight Activity-Based Costing: A Tool to Aid Decision Making

a. Factory overhead
b. Contribution margin analysis
c. Profit center
d. Cost driver

5. A _____ is a tangible input for a product manufactured/Service provided, like labor or material. For example a cloth manufacturing firm requires some amount of predetermined labor and predetermined raw material for any amount of cloth being manufactured. The cost of employing labor can be directly fixed as 'per man per hour' or 'per man per day', so the labor is a _____ as you can directly associate cost with it.

a. 3M Company
b. Round-tripping
c. Residual value
d. Cost object

6. The U.S. _____ is an independent agency of the United States government which holds primary responsibility for enforcing the federal securities laws and regulating the securities industry, the nation's stock and options exchanges, and other electronic securities markets. The SEC was created by section 4 of the Securities Exchange Act of 1934 (now codified as 15 U.S.C. ÂÂ§ 78d and commonly referred to as the 1934 Act.)

a. BNSF Railway
b. 3M Company
c. BMC Software, Inc.
d. Securities and Exchange Commission

7. A _____ is a fungible, negotiable instrument representing financial value. they are broadly categorized into debt securities (such as banknotes, bonds and debentures), and equity securities; e.g., common stocks. The company or other entity issuing the _____ is called the issuer.

a. Tracking stock
b. BMC Software, Inc.
c. 3M Company
d. Security

8. _____ is a process of attributing cost to particular cost centres. For example the wage of the driver of the purchasing department can be allocated to the purchasing department cost centre. It is not necessary to share the wage cost over several different cost centers.

a. Cost allocation
b. Cost of quality
c. Cost accounting
d. Variable cost

9. A _____, also client, buyer or purchaser is the buyer or user of the paid products of an individual or organization, mostly called the supplier or seller. This is typically through purchasing or renting goods or services.
   a. BMC Software, Inc.
   b. BNSF Railway
   c. 3M Company
   d. Customer

10. _____ is a method of identifying and evaluating activities that a business performs using activity-based costing to carry out a value chain analysis or a re-engineering initiative to improve strategic and operational decisions in an organization. Activity-based costing establishes relationships between overhead costs and activities so that overhead costs can be more precisely allocated to products, services, or customer segments. _____ focuses on managing activities to reduce costs and improve customer value.
    a. Activity-based costing
    b. Indirect costs
    c. ABC Television Network
    d. Activity-based management

11. _____ is the process of comparing the cost, cycle time, productivity, or quality of a specific process or method to another that is widely considered to be an industry standard or best practice. Essentially, _____ provides a snapshot of the performance of your business and helps you understand where you are in relation to a particular standard. The result is often a business case for making changes in order to make improvements.
    a. Strategic business unit
    b. Benchmarking
    c. BMC Software, Inc.
    d. 3M Company

12. _____ is the term used to refer to the standard framework of guidelines for financial accounting used in any given jurisdiction. _____ includes the standards, conventions, and rules accountants follow in recording and summarizing transactions, and in the preparation of financial statements.

Financial accounting information must be assembled and reported objectively.

a. Current asset
b. Generally accepted accounting principles
c. General ledger
d. Long-term liabilities

Chapter 9. Nine Profit Planning

1. Project _____: The project _____ is a prediction of the costs associated with a particular company project. These costs include labor, materials, and other related expenses. The project _____ is often broken down into specific tasks, with task _____s assigned to each.
   a. Budget
   b. 3M Company
   c. BNSF Railway
   d. BMC Software, Inc.

2. In mathematics _____s are numbers or other things that get multiplied. In particular, see:

   - Factorization, the decomposition of an object into a product of other objects
   - Integer factorization, the process of breaking down a composite number into smaller non-trivial divisors
   - A coefficient
   - A divisor of a particular number, or of an element of a monoid
   - A von Neumann algebra with a trivial center

   In statistics

   - _____ analysis is the study of how _____s or certain variables affect variables.

   In technology:

   - Human _____s, a profession that focuses on how people interact with products, tools, or procedures
   - 'Functionality, Application domain, Conditions, Technology, Objects and Responsibility;', In object-oriented programming

   In computer science and information technology:

   - Authentication _____, a piece of information used to verify a person's identity for security purposes
   - _____, a Unix command for numbers factorization
   - _____ (programming language), an experimental Forth-like programming language

   In television:

   - The O'Reilly _____, an American talk show hosted by Bill O'Reilly on Fox News.
   - The Krypton _____, a British game show hosted by Gordon Burns, formally on ITV. Also had an American version.

a. Merck ' Co., Inc.
b. Valuation
c. The Goodyear Tire ' Rubber Company
d. Factor

3. A _____ is the pinnacle activity involved in selling products or services in return for money or other compensation. It is an act of completion of a commercial activity.

A _____ is completed by the seller, the owner of the goods.

a. Tertiary sector of economy
b. High yield stock
c. Maturity
d. Sale

4. _____ is the amount of inventory a company have in stock at the end of this fiscal year. It is closely related with _____ Cost, which is the amount of money spent to get these goods in stock. It should be calculated at the Lower of Cost or Market.
a. ABC Television Network
b. Inventory turnover ratio
c. AIG
d. Ending inventory

5. _____ is a company's financial statement that indicates how the revenue is transformed into the net income The purpose of the _____ is to show managers and investors whether the company made or lost money during the period being reported.

The important thing to remember about an _____ is that it represents a period of time.

a. AIG
b. ABC Television Network
c. Income statement
d. AMEX

6. A film _____ determines how much money will be spent on the entire film project. It involves the identification and estimation of cost items for each phase of filmmaking (development, pre-production, production, post-production and distribution.)

The budget structure is normally split into 'above-the-line' (creative) and 'below-the-line' (technical) costs.

a. 3M Company
b. BMC Software, Inc.
c. BNSF Railway
d. Production budget

7. Total _____ is a method of Accounting cost which entails the full cost of manufacturing or providing a service. This includes not just the costs of materials and labour, but also of all manufacturing overheads (whether e;fixede; or e;variablee;.) One of the main reasons for absorbing overheads into the cost of units is for inventory valuation purposes.

a. ABC Television Network
b. AMEX
c. AIG
d. Absorption costing

8. In financial accounting, a _____ or statement of financial position is a summary of a person's or organization's balances. Assets, liabilities and ownership equity are listed as of a specific date, such as the end of its financial year. A _____ is often described as a snapshot of a company's financial condition.

a. Financial statements
b. 3M Company
c. Statement of retained earnings
d. Balance sheet

9. In accounting, _____ has a very specific meaning. It is an outflow of cash or other valuable assets from a person or company to another person or company. This outflow of cash is generally one side of a trade for products or services that have equal or better current or future value to the buyer than to the seller.

a. Expense
b. AIG
c. ABC Television Network
d. AMEX

10. In business, _____, Overhead cost or _____ expense refers to an ongoing expense of operating a business. The term _____ is usually used to group expenses that are necessary to the continued functioning of the business, but do not directly generate profits.

_____ expenses are all costs on the income statement except for direct labor and direct materials.

a. ABC Television Network
b. AIG
c. Overhead
d. Intangible assets

11. _____ refers to the methods, practices and operations conducted to promote and sustain certain categories of commercial activity. The term is understood to have different specific meanings depending on the context. Merchandise is a sale goods at a store

In marketing, one of the definitions of _____ is the practice in which the brand or image from one product or service is used to sell another.

a. Merchandise
b. 3M Company
c. BMC Software, Inc.
d. Merchandising

12. _____ refers to a business or organization attempting to acquire goods or services to accomplish the goals of the enterprise. Though there are several organizations that attempt to set standards in the _____ process, processes can vary greatly between organizations. Typically the word e;_____e; is not used interchangeably with the word e;procuremente;, since procurement typically includes Expediting, Supplier Quality, and Traffic and Logistics (T'L) in addition to _____.

a. Free port
b. Consignor
c. Supply chain
d. Purchasing

13. _____s are goods that have completed the manufacturing process but have not yet been sold or distributed to the end user.

Manufacturing has three classes of inventory:

1. Raw material
2. Work in process
3. _____s

A good purchased as a 'raw material' goes into the manufacture of a product. A good only partially completed during the manufacturing process is called 'work in process'. When the good is completed as to manufacturing but not yet sold or distributed to the end-user is called a '_____'.

a. 3M Company
b. Reorder point
c. FIFO and LIFO accounting
d. Finished good

14. _____ is the balance of the amounts of cash being received and paid by a business during a defined period of time, sometimes tied to a specific project. Measurement of _____ can be used

- to evaluate the state or performance of a business or project.
- to determine problems with liquidity. Being profitable does not necessarily mean being liquid. A company can fail because of a shortage of cash, even while profitable.
- to project rate of returns. The time of _____s into and out of projects are used as inputs to financial models such as internal rate of return, and net present value.
- to examine income or growth of a business when it is believed that accrual accounting concepts do not represent economic realities. Alternately, _____ can be used to 'validate' the net income generated by accrual accounting.

_____ as a generic term may be used differently depending on context, and certain _____ definitions may be adapted by analysts and users for their own uses. Common terms include operating _____ and free _____.

a. Controlling interest
b. Flow-through entity
c. Cash flow
d. Commercial paper

Chapter 10. Ten Standard Costs and the Balanced Scorecard

1. The _____ is a performance management tool which began as a concept for measuring whether the smaller-scale operational activities of a company are aligned with its larger-scale objectives in terms of vision and strategy.

By focusing not only on financial outcomes but also on the operational, marketing and developmental inputs to these, the _____ helps provide a more comprehensive view of a business, which in turn helps organizations act in their best long-term interests. This tool is also being used to address business response to climate change and greenhouse gas emissions.

   a. Management by objectives
   b. Best practice
   c. Trustee
   d. Balanced scorecard

2. In economics, business, retail, and accounting, a _____ is the value of money that has been used up to produce something, and hence is not available for use anymore. In economics, a _____ is an alternative that is given up as a result of a decision. In business, the _____ may be one of acquisition, in which case the amount of money expended to acquire it is counted as _____.
   a. Cost allocation
   b. Cost of quality
   c. Prime cost
   d. Cost

3. The _____ is a private, not-for-profit organization whose primary purpose is to develop generally accepted accounting principles (GAAP) within the United States in the public's interest. The Securities and Exchange Commission (SEC) designated the _____ as the organization responsible for setting accounting standards for public companies in the U.S. It was created in 1973, replacing the Accounting Principles Board and the Committee on Accounting Procedure of the American Institute of Certified Public Accountants. The _____'s mission is 'to establish and improve standards of financial accounting and reporting for the guidance and education of the public, including issuers, auditors, and users of financial information.'

The _____ is not a governmental body.

   a. Financial Accounting Standards Board
   b. Fannie Mae
   c. Public company
   d. Governmental Accounting Standards Board

4. _____ is a 'policy by which management devotes its time to investigating only those situations in which actual results differ significantly from planned results. The idea is that management should spend its valuable time concentrating on the more important items (such as shaping the company's future strategic course.) Attention is given only to material deviations requiring investigation.'

Chapter 10. Ten Standard Costs and the Balanced Scorecard

It is not entirely synonymous with the concept of exception management in that it describes a policy where absolute focus is on exception management, in contrast to moderate application of exception management.

a. Performance measurement
b. Management by exception
c. Best practice
d. Cash cow

5. In economics, _____ are business expenses that are not dependent on the activities of the business They tend to be time-related, such as salaries or rents being paid per month. This is in contrast to variable costs, which are volume-related (and are paid per quantity.)

In management accounting, _____ are defined as expenses that do not change in proportion to the activity of a business, within the relevant period or scale of production.

a. Marginal cost
b. Cost of quality
c. Fixed costs
d. Cost accounting

6. In probability theory and statistics, the _____ of a random variable, probability distribution averaging the squared distance of its possible values from the expected value (mean.) Whereas the mean is a way to describe the location of a distribution, the _____ is a way to capture its scale or degree of being spread out. The unit of _____ is the square of the unit of the original variable.

a. Monte Carlo methods
b. Variance
c. Time series
d. Statistics

7. In statistics, _____ (ANOVA) is a collection of statistical models, and their associated procedures, in which the observed variance is partitioned into components due to different explanatory variables. In its simplest form ANOVA gives a statistical test of whether the means of several groups are all equal, and therefore generalizes Student's two-sample t-test to more than two groups.

There are three conceptual classes of such models:

1. Fixed-effects models assumes that the data came from normal populations which may differ only in their means. (Model 1)
2. Random effects models assume that the data describe a hierarchy of different populations whose differences are constrained by the hierarchy. (Model 2)
3. Mixed-effect models describe situations where both fixed and random effects are present. (Model 3)

In practice, there are several types of ANOVA depending on the number of treatments and the way they are applied to the subjects in the experiment:

- One-way ANOVA is used to test for differences among two or more independent groups. Typically, however, the one-way ANOVA is used to test for differences among at least three groups, since the two-group case can be covered by a T-test (Gossett, 1908.)

a. Intergenerational equity
b. Open database connectivity
c. IMF
d. Analysis of variance

8. _____ in economics and business is the result of an exchange and from that trade we assign a numerical monetary value to a good, service or asset. If Alice trades Bob 4 apples for an orange, the _____ of an orange is 4 apples. Inversely, the _____ of an apple is 1/4 oranges.
   a. Transactional Net Margin Method
   b. Price
   c. Price discrimination
   d. Discounts and allowances

9. Government _____ are designed to show nonfinancial aspects of government operations. For example, a government financial report might include the number of arrests, number of convictions by crime category as well as the change (i.e., increase or decrease) in crime rate. Government _____ usually provide data on environmental conditions, education and conditions of streets and roads.
   a. BMC Software, Inc.
   b. Performance reports
   c. 3M Company
   d. BNSF Railway

Chapter 10. Ten Standard Costs and the Balanced Scorecard

10. In business, _____, Overhead cost or _____ expense refers to an ongoing expense of operating a business. The term _____ is usually used to group expenses that are necessary to the continued functioning of the business, but do not directly generate profits.

_____ expenses are all costs on the income statement except for direct labor and direct materials.

   a. Intangible assets
   b. Overhead
   c. ABC Television Network
   d. AIG

11. The materials _____ is computed as follows:

   Vmp = (Actual Unit Cost - Standard Unit Cost) * Actual Quantity Purchased

or

   Vmp = (Actual Quantity Purchased * Actual Unit Cost) - (Actual Quantity Purchased * Standard Unit Cost.)

When the Actual Materials Price is higher than the Standard Materials Price, the variance is said to be unfavorable, since the Actual price paid on materials purchased is greater than the allowed standard. The variance is said to be favorable when the Standard materials Price is higher than the Actual Materials Price, since less money was spent in purchasing the materials than the allowed standard.

   a. Consolidated financial statements
   b. Fund accounting
   c. Price variance
   d. Liquidating dividend

12. _____ is a common concept in economics, and gives rise to derived concepts such as consumer debt. Generally _____ is defined by opposition to production. But the precise definition can vary because different schools of economists define production quite differently.
   a. Yield
   b. Mitigating Control
   c. Starving the beast
   d. Consumption

Chapter 10. Ten Standard Costs and the Balanced Scorecard

13. The International Organization for Standardization (Organisation internationale de normalisation), widely known as _____ , is an international-standard-setting body composed of representatives from various national standards organizations. Founded on 23 February 1947, the organization promulgates worldwide proprietary industrial and commercial standards. It is headquartered in Geneva, Switzerland.
    a. ABC Television Network
    b. AIG
    c. AMEX
    d. ISO

14. An _____ is a term used in behavioral economics to describe those types of behaviors that impose costs on a person in the long-run that are not taken into account when making decisions in the present. Classical Economics discourages government from creating legislation that targets internalities, because it is assumed that the consumer takes these personal costs into account when paying for the good that causes the _____. For example, cigarettes should be taxed because of the negative consumption externalities that they impose, such as second-hand smoke, not because the smoker harms him or herself by smoking.
    a. Authorised capital
    b. Operating budget
    c. Inventory turnover ratio
    d. Internality

15. The _____ is the United States federal government agency that collects taxes and enforces the internal revenue laws. It is an agency within the U.S. Dept of the treasury responsible for interpretation and application of Federal tax law. The official U.S. Treasury regulations provide (in part):

The _____ is a bureau of the Department of the Treasury under the immediate direction of the Commissioner of Internal Revenue.

    a. Income tax
    b. Indirect tax
    c. Internal Revenue Service
    d. Use tax

16. In corporate finance, _____ or _____ is an estimate of true economic profit after making corrective adjustments to GAAP accounting, including deducting the opportunity cost of equity capital. _____ can be measured as Net Operating Profit After Taxes(or NOPAT) less the money cost of capital. _____ is similar in nature to that of calculating another financial performance measure - Residual Income , however, there are a few complexities involved with coming up with the elements for calculating _____ over RI such as the myriad adjustments that might be made to NOPAT before it is suitable for the formula below.

a. Internal control
b. Outsourcing
c. International Monetary Fund
d. Economic value added

17. _____ refers to the additional value of a commodity over the cost of commodities used to produce it from the previous stage of production. An example is the price of gasoline at the pump over the price of the oil in it. In national accounts used in macroeconomics, it refers to the contribution of the factors of production, i.e., land, labor, and capital goods, to raising the value of a product and corresponds to the incomes received by the owners of these factors.
   a. Supply-side economics
   b. Value added
   c. 3M Company
   d. Minimum wage

18. _____ is systematic determination of merit, worth, and significance of something or someone using criteria against a set of standards. _____ often is used to characterize and appraise subjects of interest in a wide range of human enterprises, including the arts, criminal justice, foundations and non-profit organizations, government, health care, and other human services.

Depending on the topic of interest, there are professional groups which look to the quality and rigor of the _____ process.

   a. ABC Television Network
   b. AIG
   c. AMEX
   d. Evaluation

19. _____, in law and economics, is a form of risk management primarily used to hedge against the risk of a contingent loss. _____ is defined as the equitable transfer of the risk of a loss, from one entity to another, in exchange for a premium, and can be thought of as a guaranteed small loss to prevent a large, possibly devastating loss. An insurer is a company selling the _____; an insured is the person or entity buying the _____.
   a. AMEX
   b. Insurance
   c. ABC Television Network
   d. AIG

Chapter 10. Ten Standard Costs and the Balanced Scorecard

20. _____ is a demonstration of a process -- such as a variable, term, or object -- relative in terms of the specific process or set of validation tests used to determine its presence and quantity. Properties described in this manner must be sufficiently accessible, so that persons other than the definer may independently measure or test for them at will. An _____ is generally designed to model a conceptual definition.
   a. AMEX
   b. ABC Television Network
   c. AIG
   d. Operational definition

21. _____ describes the situation when output from (or information about the result of) an event or phenomenon in the past will influence the same event/phenomenon in the present or future. When an event is part of a chain of cause-and-effect that forms a circuit or loop, then the event is said to 'feed back' into itself.

   _____ is also a synonym for:

   - _____ Signal; the information about the initial event that is the basis for subsequent modification of the event.
   - _____ Loop; the causal path that leads from the initial generation of the _____ signal to the subsequent modification of the event.

   _____ is a mechanism, process or signal that is looped back to control a system within itself. Such a loop is called a _____ loop.

   a. BMC Software, Inc.
   b. 3M Company
   c. Controllable
   d. Feedback

22. A _____, also client, buyer or purchaser is the buyer or user of the paid products of an individual or organization, mostly called the supplier or seller. This is typically through purchasing or renting goods or services.
   a. BMC Software, Inc.
   b. BNSF Railway
   c. 3M Company
   d. Customer

23. _____ is the collection, transport, processing, recycling or disposal, and monitoring of waste materials. The term usually relates to materials produced by human activity, and is generally undertaken to reduce their effect on health, the environment or aesthetics. _____ is also carried out to recover resources from it.

a. BNSF Railway
b. BMC Software, Inc.
c. Waste Management
d. 3M Company

24. Closely related to system time is _____, which is a count of the total CPU time consumed by an executing process. It may be split into user and system CPU time, representing the time spent executing user code and system kernel code, respectively. _____s are a tally of CPU instructions or clock cycles and generally have no direct correlation to wall time.
   a. Laffer curve
   b. Bookkeeping
   c. Return on assets
   d. Process time

Chapter 11. Eleven Flexible Budgets and Overhead Analysis

1. In business, _____, Overhead cost or _____ expense refers to an ongoing expense of operating a business. The term _____ is usually used to group expenses that are necessary to the continued functioning of the business, but do not directly generate profits.

_____ expenses are all costs on the income statement except for direct labor and direct materials.

   a. AIG
   b. ABC Television Network
   c. Intangible assets
   d. Overhead

2. _____ is a costing model that identifies activities in an organization and assigns the cost of each activity resource to all products and services according to the actual consumption by each: it assigns more indirect costs (overhead) into direct costs.

In this way an organization can establish the true cost of its individual products and services for the purposes of identifying and eliminating those which are unprofitable and lowering the prices of those which are overpriced.

In a business organization, the ABC methodology assigns an organization's resource costs through activities to the products and services provided to its customers.

   a. Activity-based management
   b. Activity-based costing
   c. Indirect costs
   d. ABC Television Network

3. Project _____: The project _____ is a prediction of the costs associated with a particular company project. These costs include labor, materials, and other related expenses. The project _____ is often broken down into specific tasks, with task _____s assigned to each.
   a. 3M Company
   b. BMC Software, Inc.
   c. BNSF Railway
   d. Budget

4. _____ is systematic determination of merit, worth, and significance of something or someone using criteria against a set of standards. _____ often is used to characterize and appraise subjects of interest in a wide range of human enterprises, including the arts, criminal justice, foundations and non-profit organizations, government, health care, and other human services.

Depending on the topic of interest, there are professional groups which look to the quality and rigor of the _____ process.

a. AMEX
b. AIG
c. ABC Television Network
d. Evaluation

5. In probability theory and statistics, the _____ of a random variable, probability distribution averaging the squared distance of its possible values from the expected value (mean.) Whereas the mean is a way to describe the location of a distribution, the _____ is a way to capture its scale or degree of being spread out. The unit of _____ is the square of the unit of the original variable.
   a. Statistics
   b. Time series
   c. Variance
   d. Monte Carlo methods

6. _____ is a common concept in economics, and gives rise to derived concepts such as consumer debt. Generally _____ is defined by opposition to production. But the precise definition can vary because different schools of economists define production quite differently.
   a. Consumption
   b. Yield
   c. Starving the beast
   d. Mitigating Control

7. _____ refers to the structured transmission of data between organizations by electronic means. It is used to transfer electronic documents from one computer system to another (ie) from one trading partner to another trading partner. It is more than mere E-mail; for instance, organizations might replace bills of lading and even checks with appropriate _____ messages.
   a. Electronic data interchange
   b. Electronic commerce
   c. ABC Television Network
   d. AIG

8. In economics, business, retail, and accounting, a _____ is the value of money that has been used up to produce something, and hence is not available for use anymore. In economics, a _____ is an alternative that is given up as a result of a decision. In business, the _____ may be one of acquisition, in which case the amount of money expended to acquire it is counted as _____.

a. Cost
b. Prime cost
c. Cost allocation
d. Cost of quality

9. A _____ is the rate used to apply manufacturing overhead to work-in-process inventory. It is calculated as estimated manufacturing overhead cost divided by estimated amount of cost driver or activity base. Common activity bases used in the calculation include direct labor costs, direct labor hours, or machine hours.
   a. Procurement
   b. Kaizen
   c. Sensitivity analysis
   d. Pre-determined overhead rate

1. In economics, business, retail, and accounting, a _____ is the value of money that has been used up to produce something, and hence is not available for use anymore. In economics, a _____ is an alternative that is given up as a result of a decision. In business, the _____ may be one of acquisition, in which case the amount of money expended to acquire it is counted as _____.
   a. Cost
   b. Cost of quality
   c. Prime cost
   d. Cost allocation

2. An _____ is a classification used for business units within an enterprise. The essential element of an _____ is that it is treated as a unit which is measured against its use of capital, as opposed to a cost or profit center, which are measured against raw costs or profits.

   The advantage of this form of measurement is that it tends to be more encompassing, since it accounts for all uses of capital.

   a. Investment center
   b. AIG
   c. ABC Television Network
   d. AMEX

3. _____s are parts of a corporation that directly add to its profit.

   A _____ manager is held accountable for both revenues, and costs (expenses), and therefore, profits. What this means in terms of managerial responsibilities is that the manager has to drive the sales revenue generating activities which leads to cash inflows and at the same time control the cost (cash outflows) causing activities.

   a. Cost driver
   b. Contribution margin
   c. Cost management
   d. Profit center

4. _____ are formal records of a business' financial activities.

   In British English, including United Kingdom company law, _____ are often referred to as accounts, although the term _____ is also used, particularly by accountants.

   _____ provide an overview of a business' financial condition in both short and long term.

Chapter 12. Twelve Segment Reporting and Decentralization 73

   a. Financial statements
   b. 3M Company
   c. Notes to the financial statements
   d. Statement of retained earnings

5. _____ is a company's financial statement that indicates how the revenue is transformed into the net income The purpose of the _____ is to show managers and investors whether the company made or lost money during the period being reported.

The important thing to remember about an _____ is that it represents a period of time.

   a. ABC Television Network
   b. AMEX
   c. AIG
   d. Income statement

6. In financial accounting, a _____ or Statement of cash flows is a financial statement that shows a company's flow of cash. The money coming into the business is called cash inflow, and money going out from the business is called cash outflow. The statement shows how changes in balance sheet and income accounts affect cash and cash equivalents, and breaks the analysis down to operating, investing, and financing activities.

   a. BMC Software, Inc.
   b. 3M Company
   c. BNSF Railway
   d. Cash flow statement

7. Total _____ is a method of Accounting cost which entails the full cost of manufacturing or providing a service. This includes not just the costs of materials and labour, but also of all manufacturing overheads (whether e;fixede; or e;variablee;.) One of the main reasons for absorbing overheads into the cost of units is for inventory valuation purposes.

   a. AMEX
   b. Absorption costing
   c. ABC Television Network
   d. AIG

8. In financial accounting, a _____ or statement of financial position is a summary of a person's or organization's balances. Assets, liabilities and ownership equity are listed as of a specific date, such as the end of its financial year. A _____ is often described as a snapshot of a company's financial condition.

a. Financial statements
b. Balance sheet
c. 3M Company
d. Statement of retained earnings

9. _____ is the balance of the amounts of cash being received and paid by a business during a defined period of time, sometimes tied to a specific project. Measurement of _____ can be used

- to evaluate the state or performance of a business or project.
- to determine problems with liquidity. Being profitable does not necessarily mean being liquid. A company can fail because of a shortage of cash, even while profitable.
- to project rate of returns. The time of _____s into and out of projects are used as inputs to financial models such as internal rate of return, and net present value.
- to examine income or growth of a business when it is believed that accrual accounting concepts do not represent economic realities. Alternately, _____ can be used to 'validate' the net income generated by accrual accounting.

_____ as a generic term may be used differently depending on context, and certain _____ definitions may be adapted by analysts and users for their own uses. Common terms include operating _____ and free _____.

a. Cash flow
b. Flow-through entity
c. Controlling interest
d. Commercial paper

10. A _____ is the pinnacle activity involved in selling products or services in return for money or other compensation. It is an act of completion of a commercial activity.

A _____ is completed by the seller, the owner of the goods.

a. Maturity
b. High yield stock
c. Tertiary sector of economy
d. Sale

11. _____ is a costing model that identifies activities in an organization and assigns the cost of each activity resource to all products and services according to the actual consumption by each: it assigns more indirect costs (overhead) into direct costs.

Chapter 12. Twelve Segment Reporting and Decentralization

In this way an organization can establish the true cost of its individual products and services for the purposes of identifying and eliminating those which are unprofitable and lowering the prices of those which are overpriced.

In a business organization, the ABC methodology assigns an organization's resource costs through activities to the products and services provided to its customers.

a. Indirect costs
b. ABC Television Network
c. Activity-based management
d. Activity-based costing

12. In business, _____, Overhead cost or _____ expense refers to an ongoing expense of operating a business. The term _____ is usually used to group expenses that are necessary to the continued functioning of the business, but do not directly generate profits.

_____ expenses are all costs on the income statement except for direct labor and direct materials.

a. Intangible assets
b. ABC Television Network
c. AIG
d. Overhead

13. The _____ is a private, not for profit organization whose primary purpose is to develop generally accepted accounting principles (GAAP) within the United States in the public's interest. The Securities and Exchange Commission (SEC) designated the _____ as the organization responsible for setting accounting standards for public companies in the U.S. It was created in 1973, replacing the Accounting Principles Board and the Committee on Accounting Procedure of the American Institute of Certified Public Accountants. The _____'s mission is 'to establish and improve standards of financial accounting and reporting for the guidance and education of the public, including issuers, auditors, and users of financial information.'

The _____ is not a governmental body.

a. Governmental Accounting Standards Board
b. Financial Accounting Standards Board
c. Fannie Mae
d. Public company

Chapter 12. Twelve Segment Reporting and Decentralization

14. _____ is the term used to refer to the standard framework of guidelines for financial accounting used in any given jurisdiction. _____ includes the standards, conventions, and rules accountants follow in recording and summarizing transactions, and in the preparation of financial statements.

Financial accounting information must be assembled and reported objectively.

   a. General ledger
   b. Generally accepted accounting principles
   c. Current asset
   d. Long-term liabilities

15. In finance, _____ also known as return on investment, rate of profit or sometimes just return, is the ratio of money gained or lost on an investment relative to the amount of money invested. The amount of money gained or lost may be referred to as interest, profit/loss, gain/loss, or net income/loss. The money invested may be referred to as the asset, capital, principal, or the cost basis of the investment.
   a. Capital employed
   b. Debt to capital ratio
   c. Theoretical ex-rights price
   d. Rate of return

16. _____ is a specific term used in companies' financial reporting from the company-whole point of view. Because that use excludes the effects of changing ownership interest, an economic measure of _____ is necessary for financial analysis from the shareholders' point of view

_____ is defined by the Financial Accounting Standards Board, or FASB, as 'the change in equity [net assets] of a business enterprise during a period from transactions and other events and circumstances from nonowner sources. It includes all changes in equity during a period except those resulting from investments by owners and distributions to owners.'

_____ is the sum of net income and other items that must bypass the income statement because they have not been realized, including items like an unrealized holding gain or loss from available for sale securities and foreign currency translation gains or losses.

   a. Comprehensive income
   b. BNSF Railway
   c. 3M Company
   d. BMC Software, Inc.

17. In financial and business accounting, _____ is a measure of a firm's profitability that excludes interest and income tax expenses.

Chapter 12. Twelve Segment Reporting and Decentralization

EBIT = Operating Revenue - Operating Expenses (OPEX) + Non-operating Income

Operating Income = Operating Revenue - Operating Expenses

Operating income is the difference between operating revenues and operating expenses, but it is also sometimes used as a synonym for EBIT and operating profit. This is true if the firm has no non-operating income.

a. AIG
b. ABC Television Network
c. AMEX
d. Earnings before interest and taxes

18. In business and accounting, _____ are everything of value that is owned by a person or company. It is a claim on the property your income of a borrower. The balance sheet of a firm records the monetary value of the _____ owned by the firm.
a. Accrual basis accounting
b. Accounts receivable
c. Earnings before interest, taxes, depreciation and amortization
d. Assets

19. _____ is a fee paid on borrowed assets. It is the price paid for the use of borrowed money , or, money earned by deposited funds .Assets that are sometimes lent with _____ include money, shares, consumer goods through hire purchase, major assets such as aircraft, and even entire factories in finance lease arrangements. The _____ is calculated upon the value of the assets in the same manner as upon money.
a. Interest
b. Insolvency
c. AIG
d. ABC Television Network

20. _____ is the difference between operating revenues and operating expenses, but it is also sometimes used as a synonym for EBIT and operating profit. This is true if the firm has no non-_____.

A professional investor contemplating a change to the capital structure of a firm first evaluates a firm's fundamental earnings potential (reflected by Earnings Before Interest, Taxes, Depreciation and Amortization EBITDA and EBIT), and then determines the optimal use of debt vs. equity.

a. AIG
b. ABC Television Network
c. AMEX
d. Operating income

21. The _____ is a performance management tool which began as a concept for measuring whether the smaller-scale operational activities of a company are aligned with its larger-scale objectives in terms of vision and strategy.

By focusing not only on financial outcomes but also on the operational, marketing and developmental inputs to these, the _____ helps provide a more comprehensive view of a business, which in turn helps organizations act in their best long-term interests. This tool is also being used to address business response to climate change and greenhouse gas emissions.

a. Best practice
b. Balanced scorecard
c. Management by objectives
d. Trustee

22. Just in Time could refer to the following:

- _____, an inventory strategy that reduces in-process inventory
- _____ compilation, a technique for improving the performance of bytecode-compiled programming systems

a. Comparable
b. Just-in-time
c. Help desk and incident reporting auditing
d. Fiscal

23. _____ describes the situation when output from (or information about the result of) an event or phenomenon in the past will influence the same event/phenomenon in the present or future. When an event is part of a chain of cause-and-effect that forms a circuit or loop, then the event is said to 'feed back' into itself.

Chapter 12. Twelve Segment Reporting and Decentralization

_____ is also a synonym for:

- _____ Signal; the information about the initial event that is the basis for subsequent modification of the event.
- _____ Loop; the causal path that leads from the initial generation of the _____ signal to the subsequent modification of the event.

_____ is a mechanism, process or signal that is looped back to control a system within itself. Such a loop is called a _____ loop.

a. Controllable
b. BMC Software, Inc.
c. 3M Company
d. Feedback

24. The title _____ is a professional designation awarded by various professional bodies around the world.

The _____ designation is a post-nominal award issued to individuals who have achieved a peer-based criteria of professional competency in the field of Management Accounting. Management accounting qualifications differ from those such as the ACA or CPA 'Chartered' or 'Public' accounting qualifications in a number of ways.

a. 3M Company
b. BMC Software, Inc.
c. Convey Compliance Systems
d. Certified management accountant

25. In cost-volume-profit analysis, a form of management accounting, _____ is the marginal profit per unit sale. It is a useful quantity in carrying out various calculations, and can be used as a measure of operating leverage.

The Total _____ is Total Revenue (TR, or Sales) minus Total Variable Cost (TVC):

Tcontribution margin = TR − TVC

The Unit _____ (C) is Unit Revenue (Price, P) minus Unit Variable Cost (V):

C = P − V

The _____ Ratio is the percentage of Contribution over Total Revenue, which can be calculated from the unit contribution over unit price or total contribution over Total Revenue:

$$\frac{C}{P} = \frac{P-V}{P} = \frac{\text{Unit Contribution Margin}}{\text{Price}} = \frac{\text{Total Contribution Margin}}{\text{Total Revenue}}$$

For instance, if the price is $10 and the unit variable cost is $2, then the unit _____ is $8, and the _____ ratio is $8/$10 = 80%.

a. Cost management
b. Profit center
c. Contribution margin
d. Factory overhead

26. In corporate finance, _____ or _____ is an estimate of true economic profit after making corrective adjustments to GAAP accounting, including deducting the opportunity cost of equity capital. _____ can be measured as Net Operating Profit After Taxes(or NOPAT) less the money cost of capital. _____ is similar in nature to that of calculating another financial performance measure - Residual Income , however, there are a few complexities involved with coming up with the elements for calculating _____ over RI such as the myriad adjustments that might be made to NOPAT before it is suitable for the formula below.

a. Internal control
b. International Monetary Fund
c. Economic value added
d. Outsourcing

27. An _____ is a practitioner of accountancy, which is the measurement, disclosure or provision of assurance about financial information that helps managers, investors, tax authorities and other decision makers make resource allocation decisions.

The word '_____' is derived from the French 'Compter' which took its origin from the Latin 'Computare'. The word was formerly written in English as 'Accomptant', but in process of time the word, which was always pronounced by dropping the 'p', became gradually changed both in pronunciation and in orthography to its present form.

a. AIG
b. ABC Television Network
c. AMEX
d. Accountant

Chapter 12. Twelve Segment Reporting and Decentralization

28. _____ is a term used in accounting, economics and finance to spread the cost of an asset over the span of several years.

In simple words we can say that _____ is the reduction in the value of an asset due to usage, passage of time, wear and tear, technological outdating or obsolescence, depletion, inadequacy, rot, rust, decay or other such factors.

In accounting, _____ is a term used to describe any method of attributing the historical or purchase cost of an asset across its useful life, roughly corresponding to normal wear and tear.

   a. Net profit
   b. Depreciation
   c. General ledger
   d. Current asset

29. _____ is concerned with the provisions and use of accounting information to managers within organizations, to provide them with the basis to make informed business decisions that will allow them to be better equipped in their management and control functions.

In contrast to financial accountancy information, _____ information is:

   - usually confidential and used by management, instead of publicly reported;
   - forward-looking, instead of historical;
   - pragmatically computed using extensive management information systems and internal controls, instead of complying with accounting standards.

This is because of the different emphasis: _____ information is used within an organization, typically for decision-making.

   a. Governmental accounting
   b. Management accounting
   c. Nonassurance services
   d. Grenzplankostenrechnung

30. _____ refers to the additional value of a commodity over the cost of commodities used to produce it from the previous stage of production. An example is the price of gasoline at the pump over the price of the oil in it. In national accounts used in macroeconomics, it refers to the contribution of the factors of production, i.e., land, labor, and capital goods, to raising the value of a product and corresponds to the incomes received by the owners of these factors.

a. 3M Company
b. Minimum wage
c. Supply-side economics
d. Value added

31. _____ or net present worth (NPW) is defined as the total present value (PV) of a time series of cash flows. It is a standard method for using the time value of money to appraise long-term projects. Used for capital budgeting, and widely throughout economics, it measures the excess or shortfall of cash flows, in present value terms, once financing charges are met.
    a. Future value
    b. Net present value
    c. Present value
    d. 3M Company

32. _____ is the value on a given date of a future payment or series of future payments, discounted to reflect the time value of money and other factors such as investment risk. _____ calculations are widely used in business and economics to provide a means to compare cash flows at different times on a meaningful 'like to like' basis.

The most commonly applied model of the time value of money is compound interest.

    a. Net present value
    b. Future value
    c. 3M Company
    d. Present value

33. _____ in economics and business is the result of an exchange and from that trade we assign a numerical monetary value to a good, service or asset. If Alice trades Bob 4 apples for an orange, the _____ of an orange is 4 apples. Inversely, the _____ of an apple is 1/4 oranges.
    a. Price discrimination
    b. Transactional Net Margin Method
    c. Discounts and allowances
    d. Price

34. _____ is systematic determination of merit, worth, and significance of something or someone using criteria against a set of standards. _____ often is used to characterize and appraise subjects of interest in a wide range of human enterprises, including the arts, criminal justice, foundations and non-profit organizations, government, health care, and other human services.

Chapter 12. Twelve Segment Reporting and Decentralization

Depending on the topic of interest, there are professional groups which look to the quality and rigor of the _____ process.

a. ABC Television Network
b. Evaluation
c. AMEX
d. AIG

35. A _____ is any one of a variety of different systems, institutions, procedures, social relations and infrastructures whereby persons trade, and goods and services are exchanged, forming part of the economy. It is an arrangement that allows buyers and sellers to exchange things. _____s vary in size, range, geographic scale, location, types and variety of human communities, as well as the types of goods and services traded.

a. Recession
b. Market
c. Market Failure
d. Perfect competition

36. _____ is an economic concept with commonplace familiarity. It is the price that a good or service is offered at, or will fetch, in the marketplace. It is of interest mainly in the study of microeconomics.

a. Spot rate
b. Transfer agent
c. Financial instruments
d. Market price

37. _____ refers to the pricing of contributions (assets, tangible and intangible, services, and funds) transferred within an organization. For example, goods from the production division may be sold to the marketing division, or goods from a parent company may be sold to a foreign subsidiary. Since the prices are set within an organization (i.e. controlled), the typical market mechanisms that establish prices for such transactions between third parties may not apply.

a. Transactional Net Margin Method
b. Pricing
c. Price
d. Transfer pricing

38. _____ is one of the four Ps of the marketing mix. The other three aspects are product, promotion, and place. It is also a key variable in microeconomic price allocation theory.

Chapter 12. Twelve Segment Reporting and Decentralization

a. Cost-plus pricing
b. Target costing
c. Pricing
d. Price

39. _____, in law and economics, is a form of risk management primarily used to hedge against the risk of a contingent loss. _____ is defined as the equitable transfer of the risk of a loss, from one entity to another, in exchange for a premium, and can be thought of as a guaranteed small loss to prevent a large, possibly devastating loss. An insurer is a company selling the _____; an insured is the person or entity buying the _____.
   a. AMEX
   b. ABC Television Network
   c. Insurance
   d. AIG

40. In economics, _____ are business expenses that are not dependent on the activities of the business They tend to be time-related, such as salaries or rents being paid per month. This is in contrast to variable costs, which are volume-related (and are paid per quantity.)

In management accounting, _____ are defined as expenses that do not change in proportion to the activity of a business, within the relevant period or scale of production.

   a. Marginal cost
   b. Cost of quality
   c. Cost accounting
   d. Fixed costs

41. _____s are expenses that change in proportion to the activity of a business. In other words, _____ is the sum of marginal costs. It can also be considered normal costs.
   a. Cost accounting
   b. Quality costs
   c. Fixed costs
   d. Variable cost

42. A _____ is a one-time payment of money, as opposed to a series of payments made over time.

a. Lump sum
b. Redemption value
c. Manufacturing operations
d. Trade name

Chapter 13. Thirteen Relevant Costs for Decision Making

1. _____ can be regarded as an outcome of mental processes (cognitive process) leading to the selection of a course of action among several alternatives. Every _____ process produces a final choice. The output can be an action or an opinion of choice.
    a. BNSF Railway
    b. 3M Company
    c. BMC Software, Inc.
    d. Decision making

2. _____ is a costing model that identifies activities in an organization and assigns the cost of each activity resource to all products and services according to the actual consumption by each: it assigns more indirect costs (overhead) into direct costs.

    In this way an organization can establish the true cost of its individual products and services for the purposes of identifying and eliminating those which are unprofitable and lowering the prices of those which are overpriced.

    In a business organization, the ABC methodology assigns an organization's resource costs through activities to the products and services provided to its customers.

    a. ABC Television Network
    b. Activity-based management
    c. Indirect costs
    d. Activity-based costing

3. In economics, business, retail, and accounting, a _____ is the value of money that has been used up to produce something, and hence is not available for use anymore. In economics, a _____ is an alternative that is given up as a result of a decision. In business, the _____ may be one of acquisition, in which case the amount of money expended to acquire it is counted as _____.
    a. Cost allocation
    b. Cost of quality
    c. Prime cost
    d. Cost

4. In economics and finance, _____ is the change in total cost that arises when the quantity produced changes by one unit. It is the cost of producing one more unit of a good. Mathematically, the _____ function is expressed as the first derivative of the total cost (TC) function with respect to quantity (Q.)
    a. Marginal cost
    b. Cost accounting
    c. Cost of quality
    d. Variable cost

Chapter 13. Thirteen Relevant Costs for Decision Making 87

5. An _____ is a term used in behavioral economics to describe those types of behaviors that impose costs on a person in the long-run that are not taken into account when making decisions in the present. Classical Economics discourages government from creating legislation that targets internalities, because it is assumed that the consumer takes these personal costs into account when paying for the good that causes the _____. For example, cigarettes should be taxed because of the negative consumption externalities that they impose, such as second-hand smoke, not because the smoker harms him or herself by smoking.
   a. Inventory turnover ratio
   b. Operating budget
   c. Authorised capital
   d. Internality

6. The _____ is the United States federal government agency that collects taxes and enforces the internal revenue laws. It is an agency within the U.S. Dept of the treasury responsible for interpretation and application of Federal tax law. The official U.S. Treasury regulations provide (in part):

The _____ is a bureau of the Department of the Treasury under the immediate direction of the Commissioner of Internal Revenue.

   a. Internal Revenue Service
   b. Use tax
   c. Income tax
   d. Indirect tax

7. A _____ is a fungible, negotiable instrument representing financial value. they are broadly categorized into debt securities (such as banknotes, bonds and debentures), and equity securities; e.g., common stocks. The company or other entity issuing the _____ is called the issuer.
   a. BMC Software, Inc.
   b. 3M Company
   c. Tracking stock
   d. Security

8. The U.S. _____ is an independent agency of the United States government which holds primary responsibility for enforcing the federal securities laws and regulating the securities industry, the nation's stock and options exchanges, and other electronic securities markets. The SEC was created by section 4 of the Securities Exchange Act of 1934 (now codified as 15 U.S.C. ÂÂ§ 78d and commonly referred to as the 1934 Act.)

a. 3M Company
b. Securities and Exchange Commission
c. BNSF Railway
d. BMC Software, Inc.

9. _____ is a term used in accounting, economics and finance to spread the cost of an asset over the span of several years.

In simple words we can say that _____ is the reduction in the value of an asset due to usage, passage of time, wear and tear, technological outdating or obsolescence, depletion, inadequacy, rot, rust, decay or other such factors.

In accounting, _____ is a term used to describe any method of attributing the historical or purchase cost of an asset across its useful life, roughly corresponding to normal wear and tear.

a. Current asset
b. General ledger
c. Depreciation
d. Net profit

10. _____ are formal records of a business' financial activities.

In British English, including United Kingdom company law, _____ are often referred to as accounts, although the term _____ is also used, particularly by accountants.

_____ provide an overview of a business' financial condition in both short and long term.

a. 3M Company
b. Statement of retained earnings
c. Notes to the financial statements
d. Financial statements

11. In economics, _____ are business expenses that are not dependent on the activities of the business They tend to be time-related, such as salaries or rents being paid per month. This is in contrast to variable costs, which are volume-related (and are paid per quantity.)

In management accounting, _____ are defined as expenses that do not change in proportion to the activity of a business, within the relevant period or scale of production.

Chapter 13. Thirteen Relevant Costs for Decision Making

a. Marginal cost
b. Cost of quality
c. Cost accounting
d. Fixed costs

12. In financial accounting, a _____ or Statement of cash flows is a financial statement that shows a company's flow of cash. The money coming into the business is called cash inflow, and money going out from the business is called cash outflow. The statement shows how changes in balance sheet and income accounts affect cash and cash equivalents, and breaks the analysis down to operating, investing, and financing activities.

a. 3M Company
b. BNSF Railway
c. BMC Software, Inc.
d. Cash flow statement

13. In financial accounting, a _____ or statement of financial position is a summary of a person's or organization's balances. Assets, liabilities and ownership equity are listed as of a specific date, such as the end of its financial year. A _____ is often described as a snapshot of a company's financial condition.

a. Financial statements
b. 3M Company
c. Statement of retained earnings
d. Balance sheet

14. _____ is the balance of the amounts of cash being received and paid by a business during a defined period of time, sometimes tied to a specific project. Measurement of _____ can be used

- to evaluate the state or performance of a business or project.
- to determine problems with liquidity. Being profitable does not necessarily mean being liquid. A company can fail because of a shortage of cash, even while profitable.
- to project rate of returns. The time of _____s into and out of projects are used as inputs to financial models such as internal rate of return, and net present value.
- to examine income or growth of a business when it is believed that accrual accounting concepts do not represent economic realities. Alternately, _____ can be used to 'validate' the net income generated by accrual accounting.

_____ as a generic term may be used differently depending on context, and certain _____ definitions may be adapted by analysts and users for their own uses. Common terms include operating _____ and free _____.

Chapter 13. Thirteen Relevant Costs for Decision Making

a. Flow-through entity
b. Controlling interest
c. Cash flow
d. Commercial paper

15. _____ is a company's financial statement that indicates how the revenue is transformed into the net income The purpose of the _____ is to show managers and investors whether the company made or lost money during the period being reported.

The important thing to remember about an _____ is that it represents a period of time.

a. AIG
b. AMEX
c. ABC Television Network
d. Income statement

16. Employment is a contract between two parties, one being the employer and the other being the _____. An _____ may be defined as: 'A person in the service of another under any contract of hire, express or implied, oral or written, where the employer has the power or right to control and direct the _____ in the material details of how the work is to be performed.' Black's Law Dictionary page 471 (5th ed. 1979.)

a. ABC Television Network
b. AIG
c. AMEX
d. Employee

17. _____ are made by investors and investment managers.

Investors commonly perform investment analysis by making use of fundamental analysis, technical analysis and gut feel.

_____ are often supported by decision tools.

a. Investment decisions
b. Incremental capital-output ratio
c. AIG
d. ABC Television Network

Chapter 13. Thirteen Relevant Costs for Decision Making

18. _____ or economic opportunity loss is the value of the next best alternative foregone as the result of making a decision. _____ analysis is an important part of a company's decision-making processes but is not treated as an actual cost in any financial statement. The next best thing that a person can engage in is referred to as the _____ of doing the best thing and ignoring the next best thing to be done.
   a. Opportunity cost
   b. AIG
   c. Inflation
   d. ABC Television Network

19. _____ is subcontracting a process, such as product design or manufacturing, to a third-party company. The decision to outsource is often made in the interest of lowering cost or making better use of time and energy costs, redirecting or conserving energy directed at the competencies of a particular business, or to make more efficient use of land, labor, capital, (information) technology and resources. _____ became part of the business lexicon during the 1980s.
   a. US Airways, Inc.
   b. USA Today
   c. Economic Growth and Tax Relief Reconciliation Act of 2001
   d. Outsourcing

20. The phrase _____, according to the Organization for Economic Co-operation and Development, refers to 'creative work undertaken on a systematic basis in order to increase the stock of knowledge, including knowledge of man, culture and society, and the use of this stock of knowledge to devise new applications [sic]'

New product design and development is more than often a crucial factor in the survival of a company. In an industry that is fast changing, firms must continually revise their design and range of products. This is necessary due to continuous technology change and development as well as other competitors and the changing preference of customers.

   a. BNSF Railway
   b. 3M Company
   c. Research and development
   d. BMC Software, Inc.

21. In cost-volume-profit analysis, a form of management accounting, _____ is the marginal profit per unit sale. It is a useful quantity in carrying out various calculations, and can be used as a measure of operating leverage.

The Total _____ is Total Revenue (TR, or Sales) minus Total Variable Cost (TVC):

   Tcontribution margin = TR − TVC

The Unit _____ (C) is Unit Revenue (Price, P) minus Unit Variable Cost (V):

C = P − V

The _____ Ratio is the percentage of Contribution over Total Revenue, which can be calculated from the unit contribution over unit price or total contribution over Total Revenue:

$$\frac{C}{P} = \frac{P-V}{P} = \frac{\text{Unit Contribution Margin}}{\text{Price}} = \frac{\text{Total Contribution Margin}}{\text{Total Revenue}}$$

For instance, if the price is $10 and the unit variable cost is $2, then the unit _____ is $8, and the _____ ratio is $8/$10 = 80%.

a. Factory overhead
b. Profit center
c. Contribution margin
d. Cost management

22. _____ is an overall management philosophy introduced by Dr. Eliyahu M. Goldratt in his 1984 book titled The Goal, that is geared to help organizations continually achieve their goal. The title comes from the contention that any manageable system is limited in achieving more of its goal by a very small number of constraints, and that there is always at least one constraint. The _____ process seeks to identify the constraint and restructure the rest of the organization around it, through the use of the Five Focusing Steps.
a. Lean manufacturing
b. Theory of Constraints
c. Lean production
d. Six Sigma

23. In mathematics, _____ is a technique for optimization of a linear objective function, subject to linear equality and linear inequality constraints. Informally, _____ determines the way to achieve the best outcome (such as maximum profit or lowest cost) in a given mathematical model and given some list of requirements represented as linear equations.

More formally, given a polytope (for example, a polygon or a polyhedron), and a real-valued affine function

$$f(x_1, x_2, \ldots, x_n) = c_1 x_1 + c_2 x_2 + \cdots + c_n x_n + d$$

defined on this polytope, a _____ method will find a point in the polytope where this function has the smallest (or largest) value.

Chapter 13. Thirteen Relevant Costs for Decision Making   93

  a. 3M Company
  b. Linear programming
  c. BMC Software, Inc.
  d. BNSF Railway

24. Procter is a surname, and may also refer to:

   - Bryan Waller Procter (pseud. Barry Cornwall), English poet
   - Goodwin Procter, American law firm
   - _____, consumer products multinational

  a. Welfare
  b. Procter ' Gamble
  c. Markup
  d. Screening

25. Transport or _____ is the movement of people and goods from one location to another. Transport is performed by various modes, such as air, rail, road, water, cable, pipeline and space. The field can be divided into infrastructure, vehicles, and operations.
  a. 3M Company
  b. BMC Software, Inc.
  c. BNSF Railway
  d. Transportation

26. Project _____: The project _____ is a prediction of the costs associated with a particular company project. These costs include labor, materials, and other related expenses. The project _____ is often broken down into specific tasks, with task _____s assigned to each.
  a. Budget
  b. 3M Company
  c. BNSF Railway
  d. BMC Software, Inc.

27. The _____ is a concept from business management that was first described and popularized by Michael Porter in his 1985 best-seller, Competitive Advantage: Creating and Sustaining Superior Performance.

A _____ is a chain of activities. Products pass through all activities of the chain in order and at each activity the product gains some value.

a. Value chain
b. Market segmentation
c. Customer relationship management
d. Product differentiation

28. In business, _____, Overhead cost or _____ expense refers to an ongoing expense of operating a business. The term _____ is usually used to group expenses that are necessary to the continued functioning of the business, but do not directly generate profits.

_____ expenses are all costs on the income statement except for direct labor and direct materials.

a. AIG
b. Overhead
c. Intangible assets
d. ABC Television Network

29. In microeconomics and management, the term _____ describes a style of management control. Vertically integrated companies are united through a hierarchy with a common owner. Usually each member of the hierarchy produces a different product or (market-specific) service, and the products combine to satisfy a common need.
a. 3M Company
b. BNSF Railway
c. BMC Software, Inc.
d. Vertical integration

Chapter 14. Fourteen Capital Budgeting Decisions

1. In economics, _____ or _____ goods or real _____ refers to factors of production used to create goods or services that are not themselves significantly consumed (though they may depreciate) in the production process. _____ goods may be acquired with money or financial _____. In finance and accounting, _____ generally refers to financial wealth, especially that used to start or maintain a business.
    a. Vyborg Appeal
    b. Disclosure
    c. Screening
    d. Capital

2. _____ is the planning process used to determine whether a firm's long term investments such as new machinery, replacement machinery, new plants, new products, and research development projects are worth pursuing. It is budget for major capital, or investment, expenditures.

    Many formal methods are used in _____, including the techniques such as

    - Net present value
    - Profitability index
    - Internal rate of return
    - Modified Internal Rate of Return
    - Equivalent annuity

    These methods use the incremental cash flows from each potential investment, or project. Techniques based on accounting earnings and accounting rules are sometimes used - though economists consider this to be improper - such as the accounting rate of return, and 'return on investment.' Simplified and hybrid methods are used as well, such as payback period and discounted payback period.

    a. Gross profit
    b. Cash flow
    c. Preferred stock
    d. Capital budgeting

3. In finance, the _____ approach describes a method of valuing a project, company, or asset using the concepts of the time value of money. All future cash flows are estimated and discounted to give their present values. The discount rate used is generally the appropriate WACC, that reflects the risk of the cashflows.
    a. 3M Company
    b. Discounted cash flow
    c. Future value
    d. Net present value

Chapter 14. Fourteen Capital Budgeting Decisions

4. _____, in general, is the investigation of a great number of something (for instance, people) looking for those with a particular problem or feature. One example is at an airport, where many bags get x-rayed to try to detect any which may contain weapons or explosives. People are also screened going through a metal detector.

   a. Capital
   b. General partner
   c. Screening
   d. Pay-as-you-go

5. Simply put, _____ is the value of money figuring in a given amount of interest for a given amount of time. For example 100 dollars of todays money held for a year at 5 percent interest is worth 105 dollars, therefore 100 dollars paid now or 105 dollars paid exactly one year from now is the same amount of payment of money with that given intersest at that given amount of time. This notion dates at least to Martín de Azpilcueta of the School of Salamanca.

   a. Merck ' Co., Inc.
   b. Collusion
   c. Competition law
   d. Time value of money

6. _____ is the balance of the amounts of cash being received and paid by a business during a defined period of time, sometimes tied to a specific project. Measurement of _____ can be used

   - to evaluate the state or performance of a business or project.
   - to determine problems with liquidity. Being profitable does not necessarily mean being liquid. A company can fail because of a shortage of cash, even while profitable.
   - to project rate of returns. The time of _____s into and out of projects are used as inputs to financial models such as internal rate of return, and net present value.
   - to examine income or growth of a business when it is believed that accrual accounting concepts do not represent economic realities. Alternately, _____ can be used to 'validate' the net income generated by accrual accounting.

   _____ as a generic term may be used differently depending on context, and certain _____ definitions may be adapted by analysts and users for their own uses. Common terms include operating _____ and free _____.

   a. Flow-through entity
   b. Controlling interest
   c. Cash flow
   d. Commercial paper

Chapter 14. Fourteen Capital Budgeting Decisions

7. An _____ is a term used in behavioral economics to describe those types of behaviors that impose costs on a person in the long-run that are not taken into account when making decisions in the present. Classical Economics discourages government from creating legislation that targets internalities, because it is assumed that the consumer takes these personal costs into account when paying for the good that causes the _____. For example, cigarettes should be taxed because of the negative consumption externalities that they impose, such as second-hand smoke, not because the smoker harms him or herself by smoking.

   a. Inventory turnover ratio
   b. Internality
   c. Operating budget
   d. Authorised capital

8. The _____ is a capital budgeting metric used by firms to decide whether they should make investments. It is also called discounted cash flow rate of return (DCFROR) or rate of return (ROR.) It is an indicator of the efficiency or quality of an investment, as opposed to net present value (NPV), which indicates value or magnitude.

   a. ABC Television Network
   b. AMEX
   c. AIG
   d. Internal rate of return

9. _____ or net present worth (NPW) is defined as the total present value (PV) of a time series of cash flows. It is a standard method for using the time value of money to appraise long-term projects. Used for capital budgeting, and widely throughout economics, it measures the excess or shortfall of cash flows, in present value terms, once financing charges are met.

   a. 3M Company
   b. Present value
   c. Future value
   d. Net present value

10. _____ is the value on a given date of a future payment or series of future payments, discounted to reflect the time value of money and other factors such as investment risk. _____ calculations are widely used in business and economics to provide a means to compare cash flows at different times on a meaningful 'like to like' basis.

    The most commonly applied model of the time value of money is compound interest.

    a. Future value
    b. Net present value
    c. 3M Company
    d. Present value

Chapter 14. Fourteen Capital Budgeting Decisions

11. In finance, _____ also known as return on investment, rate of profit or sometimes just return, is the ratio of money gained or lost on an investment relative to the amount of money invested. The amount of money gained or lost may be referred to as interest, profit/loss, gain/loss, or net income/loss. The money invested may be referred to as the asset, capital, principal, or the cost basis of the investment.
    a. Debt to capital ratio
    b. Theoretical ex-rights price
    c. Rate of return
    d. Capital employed

12. Discounting is a financial mechanism in which a debtor obtains the right to delay payments to a creditor, for a defined period of time, in exchange for a charge or fee. Essentially, the party that owes money in the present purchases the right to delay the payment until some future date. The _____, or charge, is simply the difference between the original amount owed in the present and the amount that has to be paid in the future to settle the debt.
    a. Discounting
    b. Discount
    c. Discount factor
    d. Risk aversion

13. The _____ is an interest rate a central bank charges depository institutions that borrow reserves from it.

The term _____ has two meanings:

- the same as interest rate; the term 'discount' does not refer to the meaning of the word, but to the purpose of using the quantity, such as computations of present value, e.g. net present value or discounted cash flow

- the annual effective _____, which is the annual interest divided by the capital including that interest; this rate is lower than the interest rate; it corresponds to using the value after a year as the nominal value, and seeing the initial value as the nominal value minus a discount; it is used for Treasury Bills and similar financial instruments

The annual effective _____ is the annual interest divided by the capital including that interest, which is the interest rate divided by 100% plus the interest rate. It is the annual discount factor to be applied to the future cash flow, to find the discount, subtracted from a future value to find the value one year earlier.

For example, suppose there is a government bond that sells for $95 and pays $100 in a year's time.

Chapter 14. Fourteen Capital Budgeting Decisions 99

   a. Discount rate
   b. Process time
   c. Convertible bond
   d. Municipal bond

14. In economics, business, retail, and accounting, a _____ is the value of money that has been used up to produce something, and hence is not available for use anymore. In economics, a _____ is an alternative that is given up as a result of a decision. In business, the _____ may be one of acquisition, in which case the amount of money expended to acquire it is counted as _____.
   a. Cost
   b. Prime cost
   c. Cost allocation
   d. Cost of quality

15. The _____ is an expected return that the provider of capital plans to earn on their investment.

Capital (money) used for funding a business should earn returns for the capital providers who risk their capital. For an investment to be worthwhile, the expected return on capital must be greater than the _____.

   a. Cost of capital
   b. BMC Software, Inc.
   c. Capital flight
   d. 3M Company

16. In financial accounting, a _____ or Statement of cash flows is a financial statement that shows a company's flow of cash. The money coming into the business is called cash inflow, and money going out from the business is called cash outflow. The statement shows how changes in balance sheet and income accounts affect cash and cash equivalents, and breaks the analysis down to operating, investing, and financing activities.
   a. 3M Company
   b. BMC Software, Inc.
   c. BNSF Railway
   d. Cash flow statement

17. _____ is a financial metric which represents operating liquidity available to a business. Along with fixed assets such as plant and equipment, _____ is considered a part of operating capital. It is calculated as current assets minus current liabilities.

a. Working capital management
b. BMC Software, Inc.
c. 3M Company
d. Working capital

18. _____ expenses are direct outlays of cash which may or may not be later reimbursed.

In operating a vehicle, gasoline, parking fees and tolls are considered _____ expenses for the trip. Insurance, oil changes, and interest are not, because the outlay of cash covers expenses accrued over a longer period of time.

a. Out-of-pocket
b. AIG
c. International Financial Reporting Standards
d. ABC Television Network

19. Straight-line depreciation is the simplest and most often used technique, in which the company estimates the _____ of the asset at the end of the period during which it will be used to generate revenues (useful life), and will expense a portion of original cost in equal increments over that period. The _____ is an estimate of the value of the asset at the time it will be sold or disposed of; it may be zero. _____ is scrap value, by another name.

a. Net profit
b. Closing entries
c. Salvage value
d. Generally accepted accounting principles

20. _____ is an American magazine published monthly by Consumers Union. It publishes reviews and comparisons of consumer products and services based on reporting and results from its in-house testing laboratory. It also publishes cleaning and general buying guides.

a. BMC Software, Inc.
b. 3M Company
c. Contingencies
d. Consumer Reports

21. An _____ is a practitioner of accountancy, which is the measurement, disclosure or provision of assurance about financial information that helps managers, investors, tax authorities and other decision makers make resource allocation decisions.

Chapter 14. Fourteen Capital Budgeting Decisions

The word '_____' is derived from the French 'Compter' which took its origin from the Latin 'Computare'. The word was formerly written in English as 'Accomptant', but in process of time the word, which was always pronounced by dropping the 'p', became gradually changed both in pronunciation and in orthography to its present form.

  a. ABC Television Network
  b. AIG
  c. AMEX
  d. Accountant

22. The title _____ is a professional designation awarded by various professional bodies around the world.

The _____ designation is a post-nominal award issued to individuals who have achieved a peer-based criteria of professional competency in the field of Management Accounting. Management accounting qualifications differ from those such as the ACA or CPA 'Chartered' or 'Public' accounting qualifications in a number of ways.

  a. Certified Management Accountant
  b. Convey Compliance Systems
  c. BMC Software, Inc.
  d. 3M Company

23. _____ are defined as identifiable non-monetary assets that cannot be seen, touched or physically measured, which are created through time and/or effort and that are identifiable as a separate asset. There are two primary forms of intangibles - legal intangibles (such as trade secrets (e.g., customer lists), copyrights, patents, trademarks, and goodwill) and competitive intangibles (such as knowledge activities (know-how, knowledge), collaboration activities, leverage activities, and structural activities.) Legal intangibles are known under the generic term intellectual property and generate legal property rights defensible in a court of law.
  a. ABC Television Network
  b. AIG
  c. Overhead
  d. Intangible assets

24. _____ is concerned with the provisions and use of accounting information to managers within organizations, to provide them with the basis to make informed business decisions that will allow them to be better equipped in their management and control functions.

Chapter 14. Fourteen Capital Budgeting Decisions

In contrast to financial accountancy information, _____ information is:

- usually confidential and used by management, instead of publicly reported;
- forward-looking, instead of historical;
- pragmatically computed using extensive management information systems and internal controls, instead of complying with accounting standards.

This is because of the different emphasis: _____ information is used within an organization, typically for decision-making.

a. Nonassurance services
b. Governmental accounting
c. Management accounting
d. Grenzplankostenrechnung

25. _____ is a term used in accounting, economics and finance to spread the cost of an asset over the span of several years.

In simple words we can say that _____ is the reduction in the value of an asset due to usage, passage of time, wear and tear, technological outdating or obsolescence, depletion, inadequacy, rot, rust, decay or other such factors.

In accounting, _____ is a term used to describe any method of attributing the historical or purchase cost of an asset across its useful life, roughly corresponding to normal wear and tear.

a. General ledger
b. Net profit
c. Current asset
d. Depreciation

26. In finance, an _____ is a contract between a buyer and a seller that gives the buyer the right--but not the obligation-- to buy or to sell a particular asset (the underlying asset) at a later time at an agreed price. In return for granting the _____, the seller collects a payment (the premium) from the buyer. A call _____ gives the buyer the right to buy the underlying asset; a put _____ gives the buyer of the _____ the right to sell the underlying asset.

a. AIG
b. Option
c. AMEX
d. ABC Television Network

Chapter 14. Fourteen Capital Budgeting Decisions

27. _____ identifies the relationship of investment to payoff of a proposed project. The ratio is calculated as follows:

$$\text{Profitability index} = \frac{\text{PV of future cash flows}}{\text{PV of initial investment}}$$

_____ is also known as Profit Investment Ratio, abbreviated to P.I. and Value Investment Ratio (V.I.R.). _____ is a good tool for ranking projects because it allows you to clearly identify the amount of value created per unit of investment, thus if you are capital constrained you wish to invest in those projects which create value most efficiently first.

Nota Bene; Statements below this paragraph assume the cash flow calculated does not include the investment made in the project.

   a. Finance lease
   b. 3M Company
   c. Debt ratio
   d. Profitability index

28. An _____ is a tax levied on the financial income of people, corporations, or other legal entities. Various _____ systems exist, with varying degrees of tax incidence. Income taxation can be progressive, proportional, or regressive.

   a. Ordinary income
   b. Individual Retirement Arrangement
   c. Implied level of government service
   d. Income tax

29. _____ is systematic determination of merit, worth, and significance of something or someone using criteria against a set of standards. _____ often is used to characterize and appraise subjects of interest in a wide range of human enterprises, including the arts, criminal justice, foundations and non-profit organizations, government, health care, and other human services.

Depending on the topic of interest, there are professional groups which look to the quality and rigor of the _____ process.

   a. Evaluation
   b. ABC Television Network
   c. AMEX
   d. AIG

Chapter 14. Fourteen Capital Budgeting Decisions

30. _____ in business and economics refers to the period of time required for the return on an investment to 'repay' the sum of the original investment. For example, a $1000 investment which returned $500 per year would have a two year _____. It intuitively measures how long something takes to 'pay for itself.' Shorter _____s are obviously preferable to longer _____s (all else being equal.)
   a. Segregated portfolio company
   b. Net worth
   c. Fair market value
   d. Payback period

31. In financial and business accounting, _____ is a measure of a firm's profitability that excludes interest and income tax expenses.

EBIT = Operating Revenue - Operating Expenses (OPEX) + Non-operating Income

Operating Income = Operating Revenue - Operating Expenses

Operating income is the difference between operating revenues and operating expenses, but it is also sometimes used as a synonym for EBIT and operating profit. This is true if the firm has no non-operating income.

   a. Earnings before interest and taxes
   b. AIG
   c. ABC Television Network
   d. AMEX

32. _____ is the difference between operating revenues and operating expenses, but it is also sometimes used as a synonym for EBIT and operating profit. This is true if the firm has no non-_____.

A professional investor contemplating a change to the capital structure of a firm first evaluates a firm's fundamental earnings potential (reflected by Earnings Before Interest, Taxes, Depreciation and Amortization EBITDA and EBIT), and then determines the optimal use of debt vs. equity.

   a. AIG
   b. AMEX
   c. ABC Television Network
   d. Operating income

33. _____ are made by investors and investment managers.

Investors commonly perform investment analysis by making use of fundamental analysis, technical analysis and gut feel.

_____ are often supported by decision tools.

a. Incremental capital-output ratio
b. AIG
c. Investment decisions
d. ABC Television Network

34. _____ is the concept of adding accumulated interest back to the principal, so that interest is earned on interest from that moment on. The act of declaring interest to be principal is called compounding (i.e., interest is compounded.) A loan, for example, may have its interest compounded every month: in this case, a loan with $100 principal and 1% interest per month would have a balance of $101 at the end of the first month.

a. Trademark
b. Kanban
c. Risk management
d. Compound interest

35. _____ is a fee paid on borrowed assets. It is the price paid for the use of borrowed money, or, money earned by deposited funds. Assets that are sometimes lent with _____ include money, shares, consumer goods through hire purchase, major assets such as aircraft, and even entire factories in finance lease arrangements. The _____ is calculated upon the value of the assets in the same manner as upon money.

a. Interest
b. Insolvency
c. AIG
d. ABC Television Network

36. _____ measures the nominal future sum of money that a given sum of money is 'worth' at a specified time in the future assuming a certain interest rate rate of return; it is the present value multiplied by the accumulation function.

The value does not include corrections for inflation or other factors that affect the true value of money in the future. This is used in time value of money calculations.

a. 3M Company
b. Net present value
c. Present value
d. Future value

37. The term _____ is used in finance theory to refer to any terminating stream of fixed payments over a specified period of time. This usage is most commonly seen in academic discussions of finance, usually in connection with the valuation of the stream of payments, taking into account time value of money concepts such as interest rate and future value.

Examples of these are regular deposits to a savings account, monthly home mortgage payments and monthly insurance payments.

a. Improvement
b. Appropriation
c. Intangible
d. Annuity

38. _____ is a financial mechanism in which a debtor obtains the right to delay payments to a creditor, for a defined period of time, in exchange for a charge or fee. Essentially, the party that owes money in the present purchases the right to delay the payment until some future date. The discount, or charge, is simply the difference between the original amount owed in the present and the amount that has to be paid in the future to settle the debt.

a. Risk aversion
b. Risk adjusted return on capital
c. Discount factor
d. Discounting

39. In accounting, _____ has a very specific meaning. It is an outflow of cash or other valuable assets from a person or company to another person or company. This outflow of cash is generally one side of a trade for products or services that have equal or better current or future value to the buyer than to the seller.

a. ABC Television Network
b. AMEX
c. AIG
d. Expense

40. _____ is fixing any sort of mechanical or electrical device should it become out of order or broken (known as repair or unscheduled maintenance) as well as performing the routine actions which keep the device in working order (known as scheduled maintenance) or prevent trouble from arising (preventive maintenance.) The MRO business is seeing a major boom with the emergence of international carriers and private aviation in Asia. The MRO business in India alone is expected to grow to $45Bn from the current $0.5Bn in the next decade.
   a. 3M Company
   b. BMC Software, Inc.
   c. BNSF Railway
   d. Maintenance, repair and operations

Chapter 15. Fifteen "How Well Am I Doing?" Statement of Cash Flows

1. Procter is a surname, and may also refer to:

   - Bryan Waller Procter (pseud. Barry Cornwall), English poet
   - Goodwin Procter, American law firm
   - _____, consumer products multinational

   a. Markup
   b. Screening
   c. Procter ' Gamble
   d. Welfare

2. _____ is a company-wide computer software system used to manage and coordinate all the resources, information, and functions of a business from shared data stores.

   An _____ system has a service-oriented architecture with modular hardware and software units or 'services' that communicate on a local area network. The modular design allows a business to add or reconfigure modules (perhaps from different vendors) while preserving data integrity in one shared database that may be centralized or distributed.

   a. AIG
   b. ABC Television Network
   c. AMEX
   d. Enterprise resource planning

3. In financial accounting, a _____ or statement of financial position is a summary of a person's or organization's balances. Assets, liabilities and ownership equity are listed as of a specific date, such as the end of its financial year. A _____ is often described as a snapshot of a company's financial condition.
   a. Statement of retained earnings
   b. 3M Company
   c. Financial statements
   d. Balance sheet

Chapter 15. Fifteen "How Well Am I Doing?" Statement of Cash Flows

4. _____ is the balance of the amounts of cash being received and paid by a business during a defined period of time, sometimes tied to a specific project. Measurement of _____ can be used

   - to evaluate the state or performance of a business or project.
   - to determine problems with liquidity. Being profitable does not necessarily mean being liquid. A company can fail because of a shortage of cash, even while profitable.
   - to project rate of returns. The time of _____s into and out of projects are used as inputs to financial models such as internal rate of return, and net present value.
   - to examine income or growth of a business when it is believed that accrual accounting concepts do not represent economic realities. Alternately, _____ can be used to 'validate' the net income generated by accrual accounting.

   _____ as a generic term may be used differently depending on context, and certain _____ definitions may be adapted by analysts and users for their own uses. Common terms include operating _____ and free _____.

   a. Flow-through entity
   b. Commercial paper
   c. Controlling interest
   d. Cash flow

5. _____ are formal records of a business' financial activities.

   In British English, including United Kingdom company law, _____ are often referred to as accounts, although the term _____ is also used, particularly by accountants.

   _____ provide an overview of a business' financial condition in both short and long term.

   a. Statement of retained earnings
   b. Notes to the financial statements
   c. 3M Company
   d. Financial statements

6. In financial accounting, a _____ or Statement of cash flows is a financial statement that shows a company's flow of cash. The money coming into the business is called cash inflow, and money going out from the business is called cash outflow. The statement shows how changes in balance sheet and income accounts affect cash and cash equivalents, and breaks the analysis down to operating, investing, and financing activities.

   a. BMC Software, Inc.
   b. BNSF Railway
   c. 3M Company
   d. Cash flow statement

Chapter 15. Fifteen "How Well Am I Doing?" Statement of Cash Flows

7. _____ is a company's financial statement that indicates how the revenue is transformed into the net income The purpose of the _____ is to show managers and investors whether the company made or lost money during the period being reported.

The important thing to remember about an _____ is that it represents a period of time.

a. AIG
b. Income statement
c. ABC Television Network
d. AMEX

8. The _____ is one of the basic financial statements as per Generally Accepted Accounting Principles, and it explains the changes in a company's retained earnings over the reporting period. It breaks down changes affecting the account, such as profits or losses from operations, dividends paid, and any other items charged or credited to retained earnings. A retained earnings statement is required by Generally Accepted Accounting Principles whenever comparative balance sheets and income statements are presented.
a. Notes to the financial statements
b. 3M Company
c. Financial statements
d. Statement of retained earnings

9. _____ is a specific term used in companies' financial reporting from the company-whole point of view. Because that use excludes the effects of changing ownership interest, an economic measure of _____ is necessary for financial analysis from the shareholders' point of view

_____ is defined by the Financial Accounting Standards Board, or FASB, as 'the change in equity [net assets] of a business enterprise during a period from transactions and other events and circumstances from nonowner sources. It includes all changes in equity during a period except those resulting from investments by owners and distributions to owners.'

_____ is the sum of net income and other items that must bypass the income statement because they have not been realized, including items like an unrealized holding gain or loss from available for sale securities and foreign currency translation gains or losses.

a. Comprehensive income
b. BNSF Railway
c. 3M Company
d. BMC Software, Inc.

10. The _____ is a private, not-for-profit organization whose primary purpose is to develop generally accepted accounting principles (GAAP) within the United States in the public's interest. The Securities and Exchange Commission (SEC) designated the _____ as the organization responsible for setting accounting standards for public companies in the U.S. It was created in 1973, replacing the Accounting Principles Board and the Committee on Accounting Procedure of the American Institute of Certified Public Accountants. The _____'s mission is 'to establish and improve standards of financial accounting and reporting for the guidance and education of the public, including issuers, auditors, and users of financial information.'

The _____ is not a governmental body.

a. Public company
b. Governmental Accounting Standards Board
c. Fannie Mae
d. Financial Accounting Standards Board

11. Total _____ is a method of Accounting cost which entails the full cost of manufacturing or providing a service. This includes not just the costs of materials and labour, but also of all manufacturing overheads (whether e;fixede; or e;variablee;.) One of the main reasons for absorbing overheads into the cost of units is for inventory valuation purposes.
  a. AIG
  b. ABC Television Network
  c. AMEX
  d. Absorption costing

12. A _____ is a piece of paper, often preprinted in a way designed to help organize material for learning or clear understanding. Students in a school may have 'fill-in-the-blank' sheets of questions, diagrams or maps to help them with their exercises. Students will often use _____s to review what has been taught in class.
  a. BMC Software, Inc.
  b. Value based pricing
  c. Worksheet
  d. 3M Company

13. A _____ is a fungible, negotiable instrument representing financial value. they are broadly categorized into debt securities (such as banknotes, bonds and debentures), and equity securities; e.g., common stocks. The company or other entity issuing the _____ is called the issuer.
  a. Tracking stock
  b. 3M Company
  c. BMC Software, Inc.
  d. Security

Chapter 15. Fifteen "How Well Am I Doing?" Statement of Cash Flows

14. The U.S. _____ is an independent agency of the United States government which holds primary responsibility for enforcing the federal securities laws and regulating the securities industry, the nation's stock and options exchanges, and other electronic securities markets. The SEC was created by section 4 of the Securities Exchange Act of 1934 (now codified as 15 U.S.C. §§ 78d and commonly referred to as the 1934 Act.)

a. BMC Software, Inc.
b. 3M Company
c. BNSF Railway
d. Securities and Exchange Commission

15. _____ is the process of increasing, or accounting for, an amount over a period of time. Particular instances of the term include:

- _____, the allocation of a lump sum amount to different time periods, particularly for loans and other forms of finance, including related interest or other finance charges.
    - _____ schedule, a table detailing each periodic payment on a loan (typically a mortgage), as generated by an _____ calculator.
    - Negative _____, an _____ schedule where the loan amount actually increases through not paying the full interest
- Amortized analysis, analyzing the execution cost of algorithms over a sequence of operations.
- _____ of capital expenditures of certain assets under accounting rules, particularly intangible assets, in a manner analogous to depreciation.
- _____

a. Annuity
b. Intangible
c. EBIT
d. Amortization

16. _____ is a term used in accounting, economics and finance to spread the cost of an asset over the span of several years.

In simple words we can say that _____ is the reduction in the value of an asset due to usage, passage of time, wear and tear, technological outdating or obsolescence, depletion, inadequacy, rot, rust, decay or other such factors.

In accounting, _____ is a term used to describe any method of attributing the historical or purchase cost of an asset across its useful life, roughly corresponding to normal wear and tear.

a. General ledger
b. Net profit
c. Depreciation
d. Current asset

17. In accounting, _____ has a very specific meaning. It is an outflow of cash or other valuable assets from a person or company to another person or company. This outflow of cash is generally one side of a trade for products or services that have equal or better current or future value to the buyer than to the seller.

a. Expense
b. AIG
c. ABC Television Network
d. AMEX

1. In finance, a _____ or accounting ratio is a ratio of two selected numerical values taken from an enterprise's financial statements. There are many standard ratios used to try to evaluate the overall financial condition of a corporation or other organization. _____s may be used by managers within a firm, by current and potential shareholders (owners) of a firm, and by a firm's creditors.
   a. Financial ratio
   b. Current ratio
   c. Return of capital
   d. Price/cash flow ratio

2. _____ are formal records of a business' financial activities.

In British English, including United Kingdom company law, _____ are often referred to as accounts, although the term _____ is also used, particularly by accountants.

_____ provide an overview of a business' financial condition in both short and long term.

   a. Notes to the financial statements
   b. 3M Company
   c. Statement of retained earnings
   d. Financial statements

3. _____ is the term used to refer to the standard framework of guidelines for financial accounting used in any given jurisdiction. _____ includes the standards, conventions, and rules accountants follow in recording and summarizing transactions, and in the preparation of financial statements.

Financial accounting information must be assembled and reported objectively.

   a. Current asset
   b. Long-term liabilities
   c. General ledger
   d. Generally accepted accounting principles

4. The term _____ is a term applied to practices that are perfunctory, or seek to satisfy the minimum requirements or to conform to a convention or doctrine. It has different meanings in different fields.

In accounting, _____ earnings are those earnings of companies in addition to actual earnings calculated under the Generally Accepted Accounting Principles (GAAP) in their quarterly and yearly financial reports.

a. Bottom line
b. Payroll
c. Treasury stock
d. Pro forma

5. In financial accounting, a _____ or Statement of cash flows is a financial statement that shows a company's flow of cash. The money coming into the business is called cash inflow, and money going out from the business is called cash outflow. The statement shows how changes in balance sheet and income accounts affect cash and cash equivalents, and breaks the analysis down to operating, investing, and financing activities.

a. BNSF Railway
b. Cash flow statement
c. 3M Company
d. BMC Software, Inc.

6. The term '_____' refers to the concept of collecting information and attempting to spot a pattern in the information. In some fields of study, the term '_____' has more formally-defined meanings.

In project management _____ is a mathematical technique that uses historical results to predict future outcome.

a. Multicollinearity
b. 3M Company
c. Regression analysis
d. Trend analysis

7. _____ is a costing model that identifies activities in an organization and assigns the cost of each activity resource to all products and services according to the actual consumption by each: it assigns more indirect costs (overhead) into direct costs.

In this way an organization can establish the true cost of its individual products and services for the purposes of identifying and eliminating those which are unprofitable and lowering the prices of those which are overpriced.

In a business organization, the ABC methodology assigns an organization's resource costs through activities to the products and services provided to its customers.

a. Activity-based management
b. ABC Television Network
c. Indirect costs
d. Activity-based costing

8. In financial accounting, a _____ or statement of financial position is a summary of a person's or organization's balances. Assets, liabilities and ownership equity are listed as of a specific date, such as the end of its financial year. A _____ is often described as a snapshot of a company's financial condition.
   a. 3M Company
   b. Financial statements
   c. Balance sheet
   d. Statement of retained earnings

9. _____ is the balance of the amounts of cash being received and paid by a business during a defined period of time, sometimes tied to a specific project. Measurement of _____ can be used

   - to evaluate the state or performance of a business or project.
   - to determine problems with liquidity. Being profitable does not necessarily mean being liquid. A company can fail because of a shortage of cash, even while profitable.
   - to project rate of returns. The time of _____s into and out of projects are used as inputs to financial models such as internal rate of return, and net present value.
   - to examine income or growth of a business when it is believed that accrual accounting concepts do not represent economic realities. Alternately, _____ can be used to 'validate' the net income generated by accrual accounting.

   _____ as a generic term may be used differently depending on context, and certain _____ definitions may be adapted by analysts and users for their own uses. Common terms include operating _____ and free _____.

   a. Commercial paper
   b. Flow-through entity
   c. Controlling interest
   d. Cash flow

10. _____ is a specific term used in companies' financial reporting from the company-whole point of view. Because that use excludes the effects of changing ownership interest, an economic measure of _____ is necessary for financial analysis from the shareholders' point of view

_____ is defined by the Financial Accounting Standards Board, or FASB, as 'the change in equity [net assets] of a business enterprise during a period from transactions and other events and circumstances from nonowner sources. It includes all changes in equity during a period except those resulting from investments by owners and distributions to owners.'

_____ is the sum of net income and other items that must bypass the income statement because they have not been realized, including items like an unrealized holding gain or loss from available for sale securities and foreign currency translation gains or losses.

a. BNSF Railway
b. Comprehensive income
c. 3M Company
d. BMC Software, Inc.

11. The _____ of 2002 (Pub.L. 107-204, 116 Stat. 745, enacted July 30, 2002), also known as the Public Company Accounting Reform and Investor Protection Act of 2002, is a United States federal law enacted on July 30, 2002 in response to a number of major corporate and accounting scandals including those affecting Enron, Tyco International, Adelphia, Peregrine Systems and WorldCom. The legislation establishes new or enhanced standards for all U.S. public company boards, management, and public accounting firms. It does not apply to privately held companies.

a. FCPA
b. Lease
c. Sarbanes-Oxley Act
d. Fair Labor Standards Act

12. _____, Gross profit margin or Gross Profit Rate can be defined as the amount of contribution to the business enterprise, after paying for direct-fixed and direct-variable unit costs, required to cover overheads (fixed commitments) and provide a buffer for unknown items. It expresses the relationship between gross profit and sales revenue.

It can be expressed in absolute terms:

Gross Profit = Revenue − Cost of Goods Sold

or as the ratio of gross profit to sales revenue, usually in the form of a percentage:

_____ Percentage = (Revenue-Cost of Goods Sold)/Revenue

Cost of goods sold includes variable costs and fixed costs directly linked to the product, such as material and labor.

a. 3M Company
b. BNSF Railway
c. Gross margin
d. BMC Software, Inc.

13. _____ are the earnings returned on the initial investment amount.

In the US, the Financial Accounting Standards Board (FASB) requires companies' income statements to report _____ for each of the major categories of the income statement: continuing operations, discontinued operations, extraordinary items, and net income.

The _____ formula does not include preferred dividends for categories outside of continued operations and net income.

a. Invested capital
b. Earnings yield
c. Average accounting return
d. Earnings per share

14. _____ is one of a series of accounting transactions dealing with the billing of customers who owe money to a person, company or organization for goods and services that have been provided to the customer. In most business entities this is typically done by generating an invoice and mailing or electronically delivering it to the customer, who in turn must pay it within an established timeframe called credit or payment terms.

An example of a common payment term is Net 30, meaning payment is due in the amount of the invoice 30 days from the date of invoice.

a. Accrued revenue
b. Accounts receivable
c. Adjusting entries
d. Accrual

15. A mutual shareholder or _____ is an individual or company (including a corporation) that legally owns one or more shares of stock in a joint stock company. A company's shareholders collectively own that company. Thus, the typical goal of such companies is to enhance shareholder value.

a. Growth investing
b. 3M Company
c. Stock split
d. Stockholder

16. _____ are payments made by a corporation to its shareholder members. It is the portion of corporate profits paid out to stockholders. When a corporation earns a profit or surplus, that money can be put to two uses: it can either be re-invested in the business (called retained earnings), or it can be paid to the shareholders as a dividend.

a. Dividend yield
b. Dividends
c. Dividend payout ratio
d. Dividend stripping

17. _____ is the fraction of net income a firm pays to its stockholders in dividends:

The part of the earnings not paid to investors is left for investment to provide for future earnings growth. Investors seeking high current income and limited capital growth prefer companies with high _____. However investors seeking capital growth may prefer lower payout ratio because capital gains are taxed at a lower rate.

a. Dividend stripping
b. Dividend payout ratio
c. Dividends
d. Dividend yield

18. The _____ on a company stock is the company's annual dividend payments divided by its market cap, or the dividend per share divided by the price per share. It is often expressed as a percentage.

Dividend payments on preferred shares are stipulated by the prospectus.

a. Dividend payout ratio
b. Dividend yield
c. Dividends
d. Dividend stripping

19. In finance, the term _____ describes the amount in cash that returns to the owners of a security. Normally it does not include the price variations, at the difference of the total return. _____ applies to various stated rates of return on stocks (common and preferred, and convertible), fixed income instruments (bonds, notes, bills, strips, zero coupon), and some other investment type insurance products (e.g. annuities.)
   a. Disclosure
   b. Residence trusts
   c. Pension System
   d. Yield

20. In business and accounting, _____ are everything of value that is owned by a person or company. It is a claim on the property your income of a borrower. The balance sheet of a firm records the monetary value of the _____ owned by the firm.
   a. Assets
   b. Accrual basis accounting
   c. Earnings before interest, taxes, depreciation and amortization
   d. Accounts receivable

21. In accounting, _____ or carrying value is the value of an asset according to its balance sheet account balance. For assets, the value is based on the original cost of the asset less any depreciation, amortization or impairment costs made against the asset. Traditionally, a company's _____ is its total assets minus intangible assets and liabilities.
   a. Depreciation
   b. Matching principle
   c. Book value
   d. Generally accepted accounting principles

22. The _____ is a financial ratio indicating the relative proportion of equity to all used to finance a company's assets. The two components are often taken from the firm's balance sheet or statement of financial position (so-called book value), but the ratio may also be calculated using market values for both, if the company's equities are publicly traded.

The _____ is especially in Central Europe a very common financial ratio while in the US the debt to _____ is more often used in financial (research) reports.

   a. Average accounting return
   b. Equity Ratio
   c. Earnings yield
   d. Efficiency ratio

23. The title _____ is a professional designation awarded by various professional bodies around the world.

Chapter 16. Sixteen "How Well Am I Doing?" Financial Statement Analysis

The _____ designation is a post-nominal award issued to individuals who have achieved a peer-based criteria of professional competency in the field of Management Accounting. Management accounting qualifications differ from those such as the ACA or CPA 'Chartered' or 'Public' accounting qualifications in a number of ways.

a. 3M Company
b. Convey Compliance Systems
c. BMC Software, Inc.
d. Certified management accountant

24. In cost-volume-profit analysis, a form of management accounting, _____ is the marginal profit per unit sale. It is a useful quantity in carrying out various calculations, and can be used as a measure of operating leverage.

The Total _____ is Total Revenue (TR, or Sales) minus Total Variable Cost (TVC):

Tcontribution margin = TR − TVC

The Unit _____ (C) is Unit Revenue (Price, P) minus Unit Variable Cost (V):

C = P − V

The _____ Ratio is the percentage of Contribution over Total Revenue, which can be calculated from the unit contribution over unit price or total contribution over Total Revenue:

$$\frac{C}{P} = \frac{P-V}{P} = \frac{\text{Unit Contribution Margin}}{\text{Price}} = \frac{\text{Total Contribution Margin}}{\text{Total Revenue}}$$

For instance, if the price is $10 and the unit variable cost is $2, then the unit _____ is $8, and the _____ ratio is $8/$10 = 80%.

a. Contribution margin
b. Cost management
c. Profit center
d. Factory overhead

25. An _____ is a practitioner of accountancy, which is the measurement, disclosure or provision of assurance about financial information that helps managers, investors, tax authorities and other decision makers make resource allocation decisions.

The word '_____' is derived from the French 'Compter' which took its origin from the Latin 'Computare'. The word was formerly written in English as 'Accomptant', but in process of time the word, which was always pronounced by dropping the 'p', became gradually changed both in pronunciation and in orthography to its present form.

a. AIG
b. Accountant
c. AMEX
d. ABC Television Network

26. _____ is concerned with the provisions and use of accounting information to managers within organizations, to provide them with the basis to make informed business decisions that will allow them to be better equipped in their management and control functions.

In contrast to financial accountancy information, _____ information is:

- usually confidential and used by management, instead of publicly reported;
- forward-looking, instead of historical;
- pragmatically computed using extensive management information systems and internal controls, instead of complying with accounting standards.

This is because of the different emphasis: _____ information is used within an organization, typically for decision-making.

a. Governmental accounting
b. Grenzplankostenrechnung
c. Nonassurance services
d. Management accounting

27. The _____ is a financial ratio that measures whether or not a firm has enough resources to pay its debts over the next 12 months. It compares a firm's current assets to its current liabilities. It is expressed as follows:

$$\text{Current ratio} = \frac{\text{Current Assets}}{\text{Current Liabilities}}$$

For example, if WXY Company's current assets are $50,000,000 and its current liabilities are $40,000,000, then its _____ would be $50,000,000 divided by $40,000,000, which equals 1.25.

Chapter 16. Sixteen "How Well Am I Doing?" Financial Statement Analysis   123

   a. Net Interest Income
   b. Times interest earned
   c. Current ratio
   d. Return on capital

28. The _____ is the global organization for the accountancy profession. IFAC has 157 member bodies and associates in 123 countries and jurisdictions, representing more than 2.5 million accountants employed in public practice, industry and commerce, government, and academe. The organization, through its independent standard-setting boards, establishes international standards on ethics, auditing and assurance, education, and public sector accounting.
   a. Emerging technologies
   b. International Accounting Standards Committee
   c. International Federation of Accountants
   d. American Payroll Association

29. In economics, the concept of the _____ refers to the decision-making time frame of a firm in which at least one factor of production is fixed. Costs which are fixed in the _____ have no impact on a firms decisions. For example a firm can raise output by increasing the amount of labour through overtime.
   a. Short-run
   b. Long-run
   c. 3M Company
   d. BMC Software, Inc.

30. _____ is a financial metric which represents operating liquidity available to a business. Along with fixed assets such as plant and equipment, _____ is considered a part of operating capital. It is calculated as current assets minus current liabilities.
   a. 3M Company
   b. Working capital management
   c. BMC Software, Inc.
   d. Working capital

31. In economics, _____ or _____ goods or real _____ refers to factors of production used to create goods or services that are not themselves significantly consumed (though they may depreciate) in the production process. _____ goods may be acquired with money or financial _____. In finance and accounting, _____ generally refers to financial wealth, especially that used to start or maintain a business.

a. Screening
b. Vyborg Appeal
c. Capital
d. Disclosure

32.   A _____ is a party (e.g. person, organization, company, or government) that has a claim to the services of a second party. It is a person or institution to whom money is owed. The first party, in general, has provided some property or service to the second party under the assumption (usually enforced by contract) that the second party will return an equivalent property or service.

a. Creditor
b. Payback period
c. Treasury company
d. Par value

33.   In finance, the _____ or quick ratio or liquid ratio measures the ability of a company to use its near cash or quick assets to immediately extinguish or retire its current liabilities. Quick assets include those current assets that presumably can be quickly converted to cash at close to their book values.

$$\text{Quick (Acid Test) Ratio} = \frac{\text{Cash} + \text{Marketable Securities} + \text{Accounts Receivables}}{\text{Current Liabilities}}$$

Generally, the acid test ratio should be 1:1 or better, however this varies widely by industry.

a. Invested capital
b. Earnings per share
c. Inventory turnover
d. Acid-test

34.   The _____ is an equation that equals the cost of goods sold divided by the average inventory. Average inventory equals beginning inventory plus ending inventory divided by 2.

The formula for _____:

$$\text{Inventory Turnover} = \frac{\text{Cost of Goods Sold}}{\text{Average Inventory}}$$

The formula for average inventory:

$$\text{Average Inventory} = \frac{\text{Beginning inventory} + \text{Ending inventory}}{2}$$

A low turnover rate may point to overstocking, obsolescence, or deficiencies in the product line or marketing effort.

a. Earnings per share
b. Upside potential ratio
c. Inventory turnover
d. Enterprise Value/Sales

35. _____ is one of the Accounting Liquidity ratios, a financial ratio. This ratio measures the number of times, on average, the inventory is sold during the period. Its purpose is to measure the liquidity of the inventory.

a. AIG
b. Ending inventory
c. Inventory turnover Ratio
d. ABC Television Network

36. A _____ is the pinnacle activity involved in selling products or services in return for money or other compensation. It is an act of completion of a commercial activity.

A _____ is completed by the seller, the owner of the goods.

a. Maturity
b. Sale
c. High yield stock
d. Tertiary sector of economy

37. In economic models, the _____ time frame assumes no fixed factors of production. Firms can enter or leave the marketplace, and the cost (and availability) of land, labor, raw materials, and capital goods can be assumed to vary. In contrast, in the short-run time frame, certain factors are assumed to be fixed, because there is not sufficient time for them to change.

a. BMC Software, Inc.
b. Short-run
c. 3M Company
d. Long-run

38. _____ or interest coverage ratio is a measure of a company's ability to honor its debt payments. It may be calculated as either EBIT or EBITDA divided by the total interest payable.

a. Times interest earned
b. Yield Gap
c. Capital recovery factor
d. Return of capital

39. _____ is a fee paid on borrowed assets. It is the price paid for the use of borrowed money, or, money earned by deposited funds .Assets that are sometimes lent with _____ include money, shares, consumer goods through hire purchase, major assets such as aircraft, and even entire factories in finance lease arrangements. The _____ is calculated upon the value of the assets in the same manner as upon money.

a. Insolvency
b. AIG
c. ABC Television Network
d. Interest

40. _____, the Electronic Data-Gathering, Analysis, and Retrieval system, performs automated collection, validation, indexing, acceptance, and forwarding of submissions by companies and others who are required by law to file forms with the U.S. Securities and Exchange Commission (the 'SEC'.) The database is freely available to the public via Web or FTP, typically posting in excess of 3,000 filings per day.

Not all SEC filings by public companies are available on _____.

a. AMEX
b. EDGAR
c. ABC Television Network
d. AIG

Chapter 16. Sixteen "How Well Am I Doing?" Financial Statement Analysis

41. _____ is an open standard which supports information modeling and the expression of semantic meaning commonly required in business reporting. _____ is XML-based. It uses the XML syntax and related XML technologies such as XML Schema, XLink, XPath, and Namespaces to articulate this semantic meaning. One use of _____ is to define and exchange financial information, such as a financial statement.
   a. 3M Company
   b. XBRL
   c. BNSF Railway
   d. BMC Software, Inc.

42. _____ is the difference between the cost of a good or service and its selling price. A _____ is added on to the total cost incurred by the producer of a good or service in order to create a profit. The total cost reflects the total amount of both fixed and variable expenses to produce and distribute a product.
   a. Markup
   b. Merck ' Co., Inc.
   c. Corporate Bond
   d. Statements of Financial Accounting Standards No. 133, Accounting for Derivative
   Instruments and Hedging Activities

43. A _____ is a fungible, negotiable instrument representing financial value. they are broadly categorized into debt securities (such as banknotes, bonds and debentures), and equity securities; e.g., common stocks. The company or other entity issuing the _____ is called the issuer.
   a. BMC Software, Inc.
   b. Tracking stock
   c. Security
   d. 3M Company

44. The U.S. _____ is an independent agency of the United States government which holds primary responsibility for enforcing the federal securities laws and regulating the securities industry, the nation's stock and options exchanges, and other electronic securities markets. The SEC was created by section 4 of the Securities Exchange Act of 1934 (now codified as 15 U.S.C. ÂÂ§ 78d and commonly referred to as the 1934 Act.)
   a. BNSF Railway
   b. 3M Company
   c. BMC Software, Inc.
   d. Securities and Exchange Commission

45. _____ is a pricing method used by companies. It is used primarily because it is easy to calculate and requires little information. There are several varieties, but the common thread in all of them is that one first calculates the cost of the product, then includes an additional amount to represent profit.

a. Cost-plus pricing
b. Penetration pricing
c. Target costing
d. Price discrimination

46. _____ in economics and business is the result of an exchange and from that trade we assign a numerical monetary value to a good, service or asset. If Alice trades Bob 4 apples for an orange, the _____ of an orange is 4 apples. Inversely, the _____ of an apple is 1/4 oranges.
   a. Price discrimination
   b. Discounts and allowances
   c. Transactional Net Margin Method
   d. Price

47. In economics, _____ is the ratio of the percent change in one variable to the percent change in another variable. It is a tool for measuring the responsiveness of a function to changes in parameters in a relative way. Commonly analyzed are _____ of substitution, price and wealth.
   a. Elasticity
   b. U-Haul
   c. Economic value added
   d. Old Navy

48. Total _____ is a method of Accounting cost which entails the full cost of manufacturing or providing a service. This includes not just the costs of materials and labour, but also of all manufacturing overheads (whether e;fixede; or e;variablee;.) One of the main reasons for absorbing overheads into the cost of units is for inventory valuation purposes.
   a. AMEX
   b. ABC Television Network
   c. AIG
   d. Absorption costing

49. In economics, business, retail, and accounting, a _____ is the value of money that has been used up to produce something, and hence is not available for use anymore. In economics, a _____ is an alternative that is given up as a result of a decision. In business, the _____ may be one of acquisition, in which case the amount of money expended to acquire it is counted as _____.

Chapter 16. Sixteen "How Well Am I Doing?" Financial Statement Analysis

a. Cost of quality
b. Prime cost
c. Cost allocation
d. Cost

50. _____ is one of the four Ps of the marketing mix. The other three aspects are product, promotion, and place. It is also a key variable in microeconomic price allocation theory.

a. Target costing
b. Price
c. Cost-plus pricing
d. Pricing

51. _____s are expenses that change in proportion to the activity of a business. In other words, _____ is the sum of marginal costs. It can also be considered normal costs.

a. Cost accounting
b. Quality costs
c. Variable cost
d. Fixed costs

52. In economics, _____ are business expenses that are not dependent on the activities of the business They tend to be time-related, such as salaries or rents being paid per month. This is in contrast to variable costs, which are volume-related (and are paid per quantity.)

In management accounting, _____ are defined as expenses that do not change in proportion to the activity of a business, within the relevant period or scale of production.

a. Cost accounting
b. Fixed costs
c. Cost of quality
d. Marginal cost

53. _____, in managerial economics is a form of cost accounting. It is a simplified model, useful for elementary instruction and for short-run decisions.

Cost-volume-profit (CVP) analysis expands the use of information provided by breakeven analysis.

a. Cost accounting
b. Cost of quality
c. Cost-volume-profit analysis
d. Fixed costs

54. _____ is a pricing method used by firms. It is defined as 'a cost management tool for reducing the overall cost of a product over its entire life-cycle with the help of production, engineering, research and design'. A target cost is the maximum amount of cost that can be incurred on a product and with it the firm can still earn the required profit margin from that product at a particular selling price.

a. Discounts and allowances
b. Pricing
c. Penetration pricing
d. Target costing

55. The _____ is the national, professional association of CPAs in the United States, with more than 330,000 members, including CPAs in business and industry, public practice, government, and education; student affiliates; and international associates. It sets ethical standards for the profession and U.S. auditing standards for audits of private companies; federal, state and local governments; and non-profit organizations.

Approximately 40% of its members are engaged in the practice of public accounting, in areas such as auditing, accounting, taxation, general business consulting, business valuation, personal financial planning and business technology.

a. AIG
b. ABC Television Network
c. Other postemployment benefits
d. American Institute of Certified Public Accountants

56. _____ identifies the relationship of investment to payoff of a proposed project. The ratio is calculated as follows:

$$\text{Profitability index} = \frac{\text{PV of future cash flows}}{\text{PV of initial investment}}$$

_____ is also known as Profit Investment Ratio, abbreviated to P.I. and Value Investment Ratio (V.I.R.). _____ is a good tool for ranking projects because it allows you to clearly identify the amount of value created per unit of investment, thus if you are capital constrained you wish to invest in those projects which create value most efficiently first.

Chapter 16. Sixteen "How Well Am I Doing?" Financial Statement Analysis

Nota Bene; Statements below this paragraph assume the cash flow calculated does not include the investment made in the project.

a. Debt ratio
b. Finance lease
c. 3M Company
d. Profitability index

57. _____ can be regarded as an outcome of mental processes (cognitive process) leading to the selection of a course of action among several alternatives. Every _____ process produces a final choice. The output can be an action or an opinion of choice.
   a. BMC Software, Inc.
   b. Decision making
   c. BNSF Railway
   d. 3M Company

58. In economics and finance, _____ is the change in total cost that arises when the quantity produced changes by one unit. It is the cost of producing one more unit of a good. Mathematically, the _____ function is expressed as the first derivative of the total cost (TC) function with respect to quantity (Q.)
   a. Variable cost
   b. Cost accounting
   c. Cost of quality
   d. Marginal cost

59. _____ or economic opportunity loss is the value of the next best alternative foregone as the result of making a decision. _____ analysis is an important part of a company's decision-making processes but is not treated as an actual cost in any financial statement. The next best thing that a person can engage in is referred to as the _____ of doing the best thing and ignoring the next best thing to be done.
   a. Inflation
   b. ABC Television Network
   c. Opportunity cost
   d. AIG

Chapter 1
1. d 2. d 3. c 4. a 5. d 6. a 7. d 8. b 9. d 10. c
11. d 12. c 13. d 14. a 15. d 16. a 17. d 18. d 19. b 20. d
21. d 22. b 23. c 24. a 25. b 26. b 27. b 28. d 29. d 30. c
31. b 32. b 33. d 34. b 35. a 36. a 37. d 38. b 39. b 40. b
41. d 42. b 43. b 44. a 45. b 46. d 47. d 48. b 49. d

Chapter 2
1. d 2. a 3. c 4. d 5. b 6. a 7. d 8. a 9. c 10. d
11. d 12. d 13. d 14. d 15. d 16. a 17. d 18. d 19. b 20. b
21. d 22. a 23. d 24. d 25. b 26. c 27. d 28. a 29. d 30. b
31. c 32. d 33. a 34. d 35. d 36. d 37. a

Chapter 3
1. d 2. d 3. a 4. d 5. d 6. d 7. d 8. d 9. a 10. d
11. c 12. b 13. a 14. d 15. d 16. b 17. d 18. a 19. a 20. b
21. d

Chapter 4
1. d 2. d 3. b 4. d 5. d 6. b 7. d 8. b 9. d 10. d
11. b 12. b 13. a 14. a 15. a

Chapter 5
1. b 2. d 3. b 4. d 5. d 6. b 7. a 8. d 9. c 10. d
11. c 12. c 13. d 14. d 15. d

Chapter 6
1. a 2. a 3. c 4. d 5. d 6. d 7. b 8. d 9. d 10. d
11. d 12. a 13. b 14. d

Chapter 7
1. c 2. a 3. d 4. a 5. d 6. d 7. b 8. c 9. d 10. d
11. a 12. d 13. d 14. b 15. d 16. d 17. a 18. a 19. d

Chapter 8
1. d 2. d 3. a 4. d 5. d 6. d 7. d 8. a 9. d 10. d
11. b 12. b

Chapter 9
1. a 2. d 3. d 4. d 5. c 6. d 7. d 8. d 9. a 10. c
11. d 12. d 13. d 14. c

Chapter 10
1. d 2. d 3. a 4. b 5. c 6. b 7. d 8. b 9. b 10. b
11. c 12. d 13. d 14. d 15. c 16. d 17. b 18. d 19. b 20. d
21. d 22. d 23. c 24. d

ANSWER KEY

Chapter 11
    1. d   2. b   3. d   4. d   5. c   6. a   7. a   8. a   9. d

Chapter 12
    1. a   2. a   3. d   4. a   5. d   6. d   7. b   8. b   9. a   10. d
    11. d   12. d   13. b   14. b   15. d   16. a   17. d   18. d   19. a   20. d
    21. b   22. b   23. d   24. d   25. c   26. c   27. d   28. b   29. b   30. d
    31. b   32. d   33. d   34. b   35. b   36. d   37. d   38. c   39. c   40. d
    41. d   42. a

Chapter 13
    1. d   2. d   3. d   4. a   5. d   6. a   7. d   8. b   9. c   10. d
    11. d   12. d   13. d   14. c   15. d   16. d   17. a   18. a   19. d   20. c
    21. c   22. b   23. b   24. b   25. d   26. a   27. a   28. b   29. d

Chapter 14
    1. d   2. d   3. b   4. c   5. d   6. c   7. b   8. d   9. d   10. d
    11. c   12. b   13. a   14. a   15. a   16. d   17. d   18. a   19. c   20. d
    21. d   22. a   23. d   24. c   25. d   26. b   27. d   28. d   29. a   30. d
    31. a   32. d   33. c   34. d   35. a   36. d   37. d   38. d   39. d   40. d

Chapter 15
    1. c   2. d   3. d   4. d   5. d   6. d   7. b   8. d   9. a   10. d
    11. d   12. c   13. d   14. d   15. d   16. c   17. a

Chapter 16
    1. a   2. d   3. d   4. d   5. b   6. d   7. d   8. c   9. d   10. b
    11. c   12. c   13. d   14. b   15. d   16. b   17. b   18. b   19. d   20. a
    21. c   22. b   23. d   24. a   25. b   26. d   27. c   28. c   29. a   30. d
    31. c   32. a   33. d   34. c   35. c   36. b   37. d   38. a   39. d   40. b
    41. b   42. a   43. c   44. d   45. a   46. d   47. a   48. d   49. d   50. d
    51. c   52. b   53. c   54. d   55. d   56. d   57. b   58. d   59. c